A JOURNEY
OF GIVING

A JOURNEY OF GIVING

The Life of Jack Edward Fruth, R.Ph.

Angie Johnson, R.Ph.

iUniverse, Inc.
Bloomington

A Journey of Giving
The Life of Jack Edward Fruth, R.Ph.

iUniverse books may be ordered through booksellers or by contacting:

iUniverse
1663 Liberty Drive
Bloomington, IN 47403
www.iuniverse.com
1-800-Authors (1-800-288-4677)

Because of the dynamic nature of the Internet, any web addresses or links contained in this book may have changed since publication and may no longer be valid. The views expressed in this work are solely those of the author and do not necessarily reflect the views of the publisher, and the publisher hereby disclaims any responsibility for them.

Any people depicted in stock imagery provided by Thinkstock are models, and such images are being used for illustrative purposes only.
Certain stock imagery © Thinkstock.

ISBN: 978-1-4620-8361-9 (sc)
ISBN: 978-1-4620-8363-3 (hc)
ISBN: 978-1-4620-8362-6 (ebk)

Library of Congress Control Number: 2011963233

Printed in the United States of America

iUniverse rev. date: 01/13/2012

CONTENTS

Jack Edward Fruth, ten years old, walking in Charleston, West Virginia, 1938

In celebration of ~

Unconditional love,

And endearing achievements,

This is the life of

Jack E. Fruth.

For Frances "Babs" Fruth, loving wife and mother.

The Oath Of A Pharmacist

"I promise to devote myself to a lifetime of service to others through the profession of pharmacy.

In fulfilling this vow:

- I will consider the welfare of humanity and relief of suffering my primary concerns.
- I will apply my knowledge, experience, and skills to the best of my ability to assure optimal outcomes for my patients.
- I will respect and protect all personal and health information entrusted to me.
- I will accept the lifelong obligation to improve my professional knowledge and competence.
- I will hold myself and my colleagues to the highest principles of our profession's moral, ethical and legal conduct.
- I will embrace and advocate changes that improve patient care.
- I will utilize my knowledge, skills, experiences, and values to prepare the next generation of pharmacists.

I take these vows voluntarily with the full realization of the responsibility with which I am entrusted by the public."

FORWARD

There was never a time in my life when I wasn't proud to say that Jack Fruth was my father. He had always been wise and generous. He committed himself to helping others and having done so made life better for the people around him. He loved my mother and was not ashamed to share that fact given the slightest opportunity.

Over the years, he tried to instill his values of honesty, hard work, generosity and practicality into his children and his employees. My father was a person of tremendous personal integrity even when that came at a high cost. I counted on him for wise counsel, unfailing love and constant encouragement.

My father's sudden death in 2005 left our family without our "go-to-guy." It seemed that Dad always had the answer for our problems, no matter how complicated or traumatic. Yet, in the years that followed, when I needed his advice the most, his voice came to me as clear as if he were in the room speaking. I had learned the answers and the lessons taught had taken hold. My father's wisdom came back when I needed it the most.

As the news of my father's sudden death spread through the town, folks began to come to the house. It seemed that every one of them had a story to share with us about a time when dad had helped. So many people said, "Your dad was my best friend" or "He was like a father to me." That pattern repeated itself throughout the visitation and funeral as people shared times when dad had done things to help in their time of need. Each story appeared to be more inspiring than the one before, and most were stories that we had never heard.

Several years later, I was asked to clean out my father's office at work. I responded with a mix of dread and anticipation. I dreaded the closing of that chapter, the reality that he was truly gone. But, I was anxious with the anticipation of what small treasures I might find from his 53 years at Fruth Pharmacy. I knew that I didn't want a secretary making the decision about what should be kept or what should be thrown away. I also knew that this could prove to be an emotional journey. I certainly had no idea the treasures that I would uncover tucked in a small drawer, unseen by anyone but my father until that day.

The contents of that drawer, in part, became the beginning of the idea that my father's life was a story that needed to be shared. In that drawer were many cards and letters from people who my father had helped over the years. Even my mother was unaware of many of the situations, which were described in the letters in that drawer. Finding those letters after three days of cleaning out the office was like finding a hidden treasure. As I read each one, I was more and more amazed and humbled. I had no idea the depth or the volume of help and support that dad had provided to different people over the years. He simply had never talked about it. He had just done it.

I began to reflect on the scripture, Matthew 6:1-4, "*Take heed that you do not do your charitable deeds before men, to be seen by them. Otherwise you have no reward from your Father in heaven. Therefore, when you do a charitable deed, do not sound a trumpet before you as the hypocrites do in the synagogues and in the streets, that they may have glory from men. Assuredly, I say to you, they have their reward. But when you do a charitable deed, do not let your left hand know what your right hand is doing, that your charitable deed may be in secret; and your Father who sees in secret will Himself reward you openly."*

After sharing the letters with my mother, she and the rest of my brothers and sisters and I began talking about getting Dad's story written. Part of our motivation was to preserve the story for our children, but as the book was being researched, it became clear that Dad's story was really bigger than just our little family. It seemed that Dad's life was a journey that needed to be shared. I hope that you will be blessed in the reading of the story of the life of Jack E. Fruth.

Daughter, Lynne Fruth

Preface

I grew up in Point Pleasant, West Virginia and from the time I was a little girl, Fruth Pharmacy has been a hometown icon. If you were sick, you went there for medication. If you needed a gift, you went there to find just the perfect item. If you were a little girl in need of a candy break, as I often was while growing up, you stopped at Fruth Pharmacy. With your bike parked out front, you ventured in among the myriad things, to find the perfect roll of Sweet Tarts and a bottle of Orange Crush. A "drugstore" that impacted something as vital as your health, yet provided something as inconsequential as sweet refreshment. That's how much a part of our lives that Fruth Pharmacy has been and still continues to be. Our hometown pharmacist, Jack Fruth, built it. He ran it. He was it.

In these changing times, his family continues the tradition in his absence. If not for his ability to build such a strong foundation, one that could remain sound in today's business forum, Fruth Pharmacy may well have become a forgotten stop along our travels.

I feel privileged to have been allowed this opportunity to take part in such an important compilation of the lifelong achievements, personal interactions, graceful involvements, and professional accomplishments of Jack Edward Fruth. Through the shared words of this book bound with heart-felt stories, together we begin a blessed reflection to reveal a glimpse into his life. His life was a true journey into the graces of human integrity that involved many people, both personally and professionally.

I want to thank his wife, Frances "Babs" Fruth, for sharing such telling stories and tender memories of the life she shared with her husband. We met on Wednesday mornings to talk about him. We would sit at a table each with a beverage and a little something sweet on which to nibble. One of us would bring the snack. I with a notepad, pen, tape recorder, and rapt attention on her and she with a heart full of expression would begin the journey down memory lane. She recalls him; the memories as clear as if it were yesterday. A lifetime of ambition, love, success, and recognition provides the fodder that lovingly fills these pages.

Their children offered candid memories of their father as a man they love, admire, and miss. His friends, business associates, employees and customers offered recollections of favors, endeavors, loyalty and service. I thank each one for allowing me the opportunity to share their personal experiences as well.

This endeavor has been a rewarding life experience for me. From a hometown Point Pleasant girl who grew up to be a pharmacist myself, he was always a man whom I recognized to be kind and gentle, trustworthy and stable. In truth, to acknowledge the accomplishments of Jack Edward Fruth would be nearly impossible to reveal in their entirety. He was a man who quietly walked through the lives of others sharing goodwill without ever seeking acknowledgement for having done so. I feel so very fortunate to share his life with you. It is with much respect to Jack Edward Fruth that I bring you his story.

Author, Angie Johnson

Angie Johnson, R.Ph. and Jack Fruth, R.Ph.

"In 1976, my class from Ordnance Elementary graduated from the sixth grade. Mr. Fruth gave each of us a bible. I just happened to be scheduled to work in the pharmacy the day that Mr. Fruth made an appearance to celebrate his 50th anniversary sale at store #21. Knowing that he was going to be there, I brought my copy along for him to autograph. He seemed flattered that I had saved it all those years. I was flattered that he signed it for me. For as long as I can recall, he was always setting a supreme example of character and often starting with children," Angie Johnson.

Angie Johnson, R.Ph.

Thank you, Peggy Ann Knight, for your tireless efforts in editing this project. As a result of your gracious involvement, folks can once again witness your giving nature and willingness to help others. Without your encouragement, input and expertise, I could not have completed this journey with Mr. Fruth.

Introduction

Jack E. Fruth was twenty years old when he entered pharmacy school at Ohio State University and among the first group of the five-year class program with thirty-two fellow students. He graduated from Ohio State University School of Pharmacy with a Bachelor of Science in Pharmacy in June of 1951. During his time at Ohio State University, Jack met Frances (Babs) Rhodes. Following graduation his journey led him to his first job as a staff pharmacist for Gallaher Drug Company in Springfield and Xenia, Ohio. It didn't take long before Jack realized the importance of being closer to home and the fact that Point Pleasant, West Virginia needed a pharmacy to service the community. Therefore, the first Fruth Pharmacy located at 2119 Jackson Avenue in Point Pleasant, West Virginia opened its doors to the public on November 1, 1952. Jack Fruth, R.Ph. was on duty. With his mother, Marjorie Fruth, by his side, they ran the pharmacy that exciting first day and took in thirty-seven dollars. His adventure in business had begun.

Along his bountiful journey, he welcomed five children: Mike, Joan, Carol, Lynne, and John, eight grandchildren, established a chain of pharmacies, impacted a community, a church, hundreds of employees and business associates, created scholarship funds, served on professional boards and educational advisory boards, not to mention the personal advisory posts he held for anyone in need. Whether directly or indirectly, he mentored all of us, in some fashion. He lent his hand, heart and resources and most often quietly so. Although a number of folks could say they have been successful, it is the steps along the way that make his climb to higher ground such an inspirational journey.

JACK AND FRANCES "BABS" FRUTH
MARRIED: DECEMBER 30, 1950

CHILDREN
MICHAEL EDWARD FRUTH 08-07-1952
JOAN ELIZABETH FRUTH 09-05-1953
CAROL RHODES FRUTH 05-28-1957
LYNNE MORROW FRUTH 06-10-1958
JOHN ROTHGEB FRUTH 01-06-1960

GRANDCHILDREN
Adrianne Nicole Trovato 03-07-1982
Stephanie Alexis Fruth 10-07-1983
Christopher John Fruth 12-16-1984
Elizabeth Lynne Trovato 11-21-85
Patrick Howe Fruth-McCormick 10-23-1986
Jack Alexander Fruth 01-05-1993
Michael David Fruth 04-06-1994
Thomas Baker Foust 11-22-1994

PART I

A Journey of Giving
Begins

The Life of
Jack Edward Fruth, R.Ph.

EARLY TRAVEL PLANS

"She was the bane of my existence," Jack Fruth.

In the late 1800s, two brothers migrated from Germany to the United States and found themselves on the banks of the Ohio River. One of the brothers, Henry Fruth, decided to stay while the other continued on by way of the river. He eventually stopped in Fostoria, Ohio. Due to primitive means of communication, the brothers lost contact. It later proved obvious that the entrepreneurial spirit of the Fruth family resonated. Henry (Jack's grandfather) lived and raised his family including eleven children in Mason City, West Virginia. One of those eleven children was Henry Edward Fruth (Jack's father). To earn a living Henry's father worked in the salt furnaces. The salt in the Ohio River District was produced from natural brines obtained from bored wells. In the early 1900s, the production of salt from this district was estimated to be 500,000 barrels per year. With smoke stacks etched against the cliffs along the Ohio side of the river yet today[1], remnants of the salt furnaces represent a more industrial past.

Though the destination of all eleven Fruth children is unknown, at least five remained close to home. Henry was one of them along with Carl Fruth, Helen Fruth, Chris Fruth and Nora Fruth Loomis. Henry, born February 5, 1891, married

---

[1]   *Today being 2011*

Marjorie Rothgeb, born July 25, 1897 in October of 1914 at the Grace Methodist Church in Gallipolis, Ohio. After marrying, they lived in an apartment in downtown Point Pleasant, in the Hooff building. The Hooff building, near the post office, was a busy hub. The lower, rear level provided offices for the mayor, Harper's Furniture and Carpets Store along with other businesses. Just out back, the Hooff building served as a livery stable with a rear entrance that faced the Ohio River. An Opera House, on the second and third floor, seated eight hundred people and included a section of seating known as "the peanut heaven" that faced Main Street. A drug store, Hooff Drugs, was located on the ground floor. Jack's oldest sister, Kathryn, was born on May 22, 1915 while his parents lived there. Three years later, his middle sister, Emogene A. Fruth, was born in 1918. The two sisters enjoyed life on Main Street and kept a pony in the livery stable. Henry, a barber by trade, was an entrepreneur and Marjorie, a housewife by choice, was quite progressive. Henry barbered to support them, in the beginning, while he later began to buy, rent and sell properties. As time progressed, Henry and Marjorie acquired several properties and along with that came tenants. Point Pleasant was a productive, economically stable, inviting community in which to locate. Just as the town's historic state park, Tu-Endie-Wei, translates as "where the waters mingle", this was a thriving town where people wanted to mingle.

As the town grew, so did the need for rental properties. Henry continued to barber and maintain the properties while Marjorie drove about and collected the rents due. Interestingly, Henry never drove an automobile. Though Marjorie did drive and took him places to which he was unable to walk, his preference was walking. Without the need to carry a driver's license or spend money, Henry never carried a billfold. He carried one dollar, in his pants pocket, to be used only for an emergency. Marjorie had attended college for one year as a gift from her Uncle, who was a math teacher. He understood the importance of an education and wanted his niece to have that experience. She did not let that year of education go to waste. Although becoming a housewife was her chosen role, she used her acquired knowledge to make a better life for her family. In collecting the rents due, she would split the total in half. She would give Henry his half and she would keep her half in her cigar box or *"the keeper of her treasures,"* as she referred to it. After all, she knew that a husband and wife relationship was a shared partnership, fifty-fifty. Marjorie was born and raised in Point Pleasant. Her mother lived on Main Street in a home that was removed some time ago and is now the parking lot for the Main Street Baptist Church. It seemed the intriguing and interesting Marjorie Rothgeb was enough reason to explain why Henry ventured down from Mason City to Point Pleasant.

Where prospering family members locate, others join. Carl W. Fruth (born in 1898) was Henry's younger brother that he and Marjorie took in when Carl was fifteen years old, after the death of their mother. Carl became a barber, under the tutelage of Henry, and the two operated the Fruth Barbershop on Main Street in Point Pleasant. Most folks, of that generation, had more than one haircut from there. Like his brother Henry, Carl did not drive. Their younger sister, Helen Fruth (born July 29, 1902), joined the family in Point Pleasant, as well, and became a beautician. Neither Carl nor Helen ever married or had children of his or her own. They shared a home together for the duration of their lives. In continuing to follow in his brother's footsteps with business ventures, Carl owned and rented out several properties in Point Pleasant.

For Henry and Marjorie, years passed and the two had planned and saved. In doing so, they moved closer to fulfilling their dream of opening their own retail store. An opportunity presented itself in Mason, West Virginia. Plans had been carefully considered and Henry had everything in place to embark on this exciting and new financial frontier with his wife, three daughters, and soon to arrive baby boy, Jack. Therefore, in the summer of 1928, the decision was made. Henry officially passed his scissors to his younger brother, Carl, and never barbered again. Henry and Carl's nephew by marriage, Louis Rossi, later joined Carl in the barbering business. He had worked at the Kyger Creek Power Plant for several years prior to changing career paths. Louis barbered in Point Pleasant for thirty-four years before he retired at age seventy-four.

The long awaited dream to own and operate their family business had arrived. But that wasn't the only thing that arrived that day. I liked to have imagined it was a relaxing day at home when labor set in and with much excitement the entire family rushed to the hospital to await the birth of baby Jack. But instead, Jack was born the very day his mother and father opened The Fountain on Main Street in Mason, West Virginia. On June 3, 1928, Jack Edward Fruth was born to Henry Edward Fruth and Marjorie Mae (Rothgeb) Fruth. Three older sisters (Kathryn, Emogene, and Henrietta) happily welcomed him. A day of celebration and excitement topped off by the blessing of the birth of a son made it a very special day.

The Fountain sold a few sundries but mostly ice cream. And after prohibition, they sold beer. With hardwood floors to walk upon, sundry dressed shelves to peruse over and personalized customer service at a lip's expression, relationships began between the Fruth's and their customers. Henry and Marjorie's business became successful. With the children taking part in store chores and services, the family grew closer and developed a clear understanding of what was required to offer proper public service to the customers in the community. Perhaps most importantly, Jack was absorbing every aspect of the business that would later serve to be of great value to him and many others.

Apart from life at The Fountain, Jack was also enduring day-to-day life with three older sisters at home. Most of which entailed a little mischief and mayhem.

Jack and Henrietta Fruth 1930s

He and Henrietta were inseparable, aside from the time she catapulted him off the end of the banister or put roller skates on him and pushed him off the porch steps. There were few times they were physically apart while growing up, but those were temporary and only until she picked him back up and brushed him off. He would say, *"She was the bane of my existence."*

Jack was a marble player. And some would say that was his second most favorite entertainment growing up next to fishing. Each day at school he would shoot marbles with his friends. He would earn all their marbles as his winnings. Many days he would have to leave school and walk home for lunch so he could empty his pockets. He had a huge collection of marbles.

Jack Fruth

And there was the dog. Yes, they had been given a Saint Bernard puppy as a gift. Their store, The Fountain, was just steps from their house. They sold a lot of ice cream and their dog ate a lot of it. Jack was remembered telling about how the dog would open wide while he and his sisters would drop entire scoopfuls of ice cream into his mouth. The family kept the dog until two years after Jack left for The Greenbrier Military Academy. Jack's dad found a loving taker one day at the store and sent the dog on his way.

With the growth of the business, the family then had the opportunity to move to a larger home in 1940. This home was in Buffalo, West Virginia. The family referred to this home as "the big house," as it was the largest and most remarkable they had owned. The Fruth family continued to work hard and build a stable foundation. As the business grew, so did the children. Jack grew out of one pair of dungarees and into another, but not to his liking. He grew up a working child. He stocked the store, cleaned the shelves and floors, pumped gas and basically did any and all chores that his parents were in need of. He became more and more proficient each year. It wasn't the hard work or repetitive chores that left Jack feeling uncomfortable; it was that he was forced to wear blue jeans. He had the stigma of being one of the poor kids that had no other choice but to be dressed in blue jeans. For him, a young man that had much pride in the presentation of things (he had turned merchandise and placed it perfectly to please his parents and the store customers his entire life), he found wearing blue jeans was a complete embarrassment. While growing up, he would frequently say, "If I ever get rich, I'll never wear blue jeans again!"

It was while attending Buffalo High School that Jack discovered his interest in math and science. By the time he had completed the ninth grade, he not only excelled in his studies but also had completed all the available upper level courses in math and science. His parents were very much aware of their son's abilities and wanted the best education available to ensure his future success. Thereby, his father did some investigating into the educational options that best suited Jack. After much consideration, Henry and Marjorie decided the Greenbrier Military School had the most to offer their son.

The Greenbrier Military School[2] was a boys-only, private, military, boarding, high school located in Lewisburg, West Virginia. Pastor John McElhenney had founded it. The Pastor opened the doors to a select group of students around 1812. By this time, it was the mid forties. The school had proven to graduate some of the best-trained and well-educated men. Henry and Marjorie believed their son would fit right in. Henry placed a call and arranged for the family to have an interview with the office of administration. Shortly thereafter a representative from the school came to their home to discuss Jack's potential enrollment. With Jack's outstanding grade point average and impressive personal interview, he was accepted. The concept of such an opportunity to receive military training in leadership, potentially serve his country, complemented with a formal education sparked dreams of a progressive future. Jack was enthused!

It was not long before Jack was packed for Lewisburg. He was a visionary, even at this early age, and always thinking to the future. His mind worked not by considering what was right for today but what was right for tomorrow and the next day. He had the ability to envision the mechanism of how initiating one opportunity could bring you closer to another and then to another. Therefore, he saw the potential of what his parents were graciously offering. Jack was intuitive and used this opportunity to attend the Greenbrier Military School as a stepping-stone. One that would prepare him to move closer to his next goal which was to attend West Point and join the Army as an officer.

---

[2] *The Greenbrier Military School closed in 1972 and the campus was converted into the West Virginia School of Osteopathic Medicine. One of the most unusual features remaining on campus today is the cannon. It still remains as a historic reminder of the former school.*

Jack Fruth, age 15, Greenbrier Military School

The Detour

"She was the most difficult sale of my entire career!"
Jack Fruth.

During Jack's first year at the Greenbrier Military School, he became very ill. Measles, one of the most contagious of all human viruses, was beckoning a victim and fifteen-year-old Jack was the target. The 1940s saw the introduction of several drugs to treat various illnesses. For the first time, an antibiotic, streptomycin, was available to treat infections. Several drugs to treat high blood pressure became available. A vaccine to treat polio was isolated but not available to the public. Healthcare was primitive but evolving. In those days, the measles was one of childhood's greatest perils. The school attempted to provide intermediate nursing care for Jack, as was available to all students, but to no avail. What had begun as an infection of the respiratory system quickly became complicated with fevers reaching as high as 104 degrees, the onset of pneumonia and vitamin A deficiency causing vision damage. Jack's parents were notified of his illness. Unfortunately, the illness progressed to the point of blindness for Jack. *It would be two more years, 1945, before the first influenza vaccines (flu) were used. And, it would be 1963 before the first measles vaccine would be available for human use.*

Sadness and confusion erupted among the Fruth family members. How could this happen? Jack, with such a bright future and giving heart, was stricken to the point of helplessness. His sisters could not consider the thought of losing their little brother that they had become so attached to and dependent upon. Henry and Marjorie were not going to let him go without a fight. In an extensive inquiry, Henry and Marjorie learned of a physician, Dr. Shepherd, in Charleston, West Virginia who had performed experimental treatments that restored vision and health to children afflicted with measles. If it had worked for other children, why wouldn't it work for their Jack? It was worth a try. Henry and Marjorie did not hesitate to make arrangements to get their son from Lewisburg to Charleston and as quickly as possible. After Dr. Shepherd examined Jack, the decision was made that he would need a blood transfusion. This transfusion was an experimental approach, at best, not only for correcting his failed vision but also impaired health. He was, at this time, blind.

With his parents and three sisters at his side willing to do whatever was necessary to help, his oldest sister proved to be the match. It was Kathryn that saved his vision and potentially his life that day. Had it not been for this procedure, it is not known how much more physical devastation the virus would have caused if not death for Jack. It took months for him to recover. During those healing months, his vision returned a little more with each passing day. He and his family made several trips from Buffalo to Dr. Shepherd's Clinic, in Charleston, to check Jack's progress. After this illness claimed one year, he returned to the Greenbrier Military School more determined than ever to complete his education. He did so and graduated in 1946.

Jack Fruth

Jack Fruth and fellow classmates

With his eyesight restored but permanently damaged, he was unable to attend West Point as he had first dreamed. That was a great disappointment for Jack. He had his mind set on becoming an officer in the US Army. He would have studied with the likes of future chiefs of staff to the President, astronauts, doctors of neurosurgery and other highly intelligent men. God worked in a mysterious way. If Jack had done so, he would have graduated in a class in which ninety-five percent of the officers who were sent to the Korean War were killed in action. There were more fatalities of officers, during the Korean War, for what would have been Jack's graduating class than any other year in history. Looking back, if Jack had not had the measles, which resulted in impaired vision, he too would have been on the front lines of the Korean War with the potential for a much different future.

Not knowing what God had in store for him, at the time, Jack used his intellect and restructured an adventurous future for himself. This life-threatening experience became nothing but a detour. He forged ahead in search of more education. His exceptional grade point average and gift in science propelled him into the research lab at Duke University in Durham, North Carolina. The Methodists and Quakers in the present-day town of Trinity had founded the University in 1838. The school, then named Brown's Schoolhouse, moved to Durham in 1892. In 1924, tobacco industrialist James Buchanan Duke established the Duke Endowment with a forty million dollar trust fund, prompting the institution to change its name in honor of his deceased father, Washington Duke. The university is situated across 8,260-acres that includes the 7,200-acre Duke Forest. The university has an impeccable reputation for educational excellence. Jack excelled in his studies at Duke. While there, he played the snare drums in the band for two years. He kept himself busy with school activities and studies but found he was unhappy. The four walls of the research lab proved too confining and lonesome. His lab work, in either physics or chemistry, would begin at 2pm and end at 5pm every afternoon. Without ever seeing anybody except the classmate on either side of his lab station, he was not content. He was without the much-desired human interaction he so loved and miles from his parents and sisters. He began to consider another stepping-stone process to change the direction of his journey. He continued his studies at Duke from 1946-1948, at which time he transferred to Ohio State University (OSU) in Columbus, Ohio to study pharmacy. With a strong background in organic chemistry, his understanding of the chemical synthesis of drugs was sharp. In the 1940s, compounds were being chemically synthesized which resulted in entirely new classes of drugs in the areas of analgesic, tranquilizer, diuretic, anti-inflammatory and anti-arthritic drugs. Jack was now twenty years old. In 1948, OSU inaugurated a required five-year curriculum; this later became the minimum requirement for all accredited pharmacy schools. Jack and thirty-one others made up this first five-year class of pharmacy students at OSU.

With his parents still residing in Buffalo, West Virginia and he in Columbus, Ohio, Jack made the trip back-and-forth to home as often as possible. Money was in short supply. The Silver Bridge joining Ohio to West Virginia, via Point Pleasant, required a toll of seventy-five cents in order to pass. For a student living a distance from home, in the late 1940s, this was a substantial amount of money. Travel was limited. Jack busied himself with academics while attending OSU. He joined the Kappa Psi Pharmaceutical Fraternity (the oldest and largest professional pharmacy fraternity in the world) and the Pi Kappa Alpha Fraternity, and remained active for years following his graduation.

It was while at OSU, that he met a particular young lady. She was an education major by the name of Frances "Babs[3]" Rhodes in 1948. He was smitten. She, however, was 'pinned[4]' to his fraternity brother. Jack remained patient and waited for the opportunity to win her over. He waited, waited longer and never gave up the hope of the opportunity to win her heart. Months passed and in January of 1949 that time had arrived, or at least Jack thought so—. Babs was no longer pinned to another, which made her available for approach. Jack wasted no time in asking her for a date. Without hesitation Babs said, "No." She wanted nothing to do with him. She captivated him, but he did not her, at least not initially. This did not result in his surrender. He was a smart man and knew what he wanted and how to get it. He waited. He tried again. He waited. He tried again. Finally, she agreed to one date. "Just one," she said. The couple went to the Clintonville Theater, which was in Columbus, Ohio on North High Street and watched a movie, *The Red Shoes*. It would be many years later before they would watch the movie again, at their fortieth wedding anniversary celebration.

---

[3] *Where did the nickname, Babs, come from? Babs was the oldest daughter and named after her mother, Frances. To avoid the confusion of having two ladies in the house named Frances, they called Babs "baby." That was until ten and a half months later Babs' little sister came along and then began to talk another year later. She could not say baby but could clearly say Babs.*

[4] *Getting pinned is when a young man takes his school pin, of which he has great pride, and pins it to the sweater of the girl he adores. It's an old right of beginning courtship. It will signify to others that she is in a relationship and off limits.*

Jack Fruth and Babs Rhodes 1949

Jack Fruth and Babs Rhodes 1949

After that first date, it would take Jack nearly a year to get a second one. Yes, a year! He was persistent and patient. Again, always thinking of what the future could hold instead of what today was missing. In January of 1950, they shared a second date and it was love ever after. She could no longer withhold herself from his persistent charm. She felt flattered that he could not consider another after all the rejected invitations and passed time. The two were pinned in March of 1950. Jack and Babs spent more and more time together getting to know one another. They studied on the university lawn and shared many a lunch and dinner. He shared his vision of what he planned to do with his future and included her as the person he so needed, by his side, to make his journey complete. They became inseparable. They were engaged a few months later on July 15, 1950. Following their engagement, Jack went on summer tour with the ROTC for six weeks at Fort Sam Houston in San Antonio, Texas. This was a long separation for both Jack and Babs. Their affection grew stronger. He returned in the fall, on September 1, 1950. The two married just a few months later on December 30, 1950. He wasted no time making her his wife, once he had *her* captivated.

Wedding Day December 30, 1950

WELCOME TO
POINT PLEASANT, WEST
VIRGINIA

"I came to Point Pleasant with a wife, a baby, and a suitcase full of dreams," Jack Fruth.

Even though the boomtown atmosphere that Point Pleasant had been enjoying was not what it once was following the war, there was still a steady rate of growth and opportunity. The Marietta Manufacturing Company offered steady employment to men in the community at a respectable pay rate and had done so since 1915. The success of the company also proved that the residents of Point Pleasant could and did offer the production of respectable river crafts constructed with top quality craftsmanship. The shipyard had forty-two acres on which a marine railway, a 180-foot by 79-foot, two thousand pound dry dock and launching way was situated. In addition to building and repairing a variety of small vessels and barges for inland service, it also constructed carbon-black plants, pipe mills and crane booms. The river proved to offer much opportunity for shipyards to transport in and out of Point Pleasant's foundries without struggle. During World War II, employment reached three thousand and the company was a respectable producer of the Army's large water vessels. It was a win-win combination that helped stabilize the economy of Point Pleasant. Barbie Rothgeb (Jack's mother's sister) was the secretary at the shipyard in the 1930s. Jack and Babs were present for the launching of the last two survey vessels from the Marietta Manufacturing facility. Babs recalled the last to launch went sideways and then down into the river. She thought it was going to sink at first! Then the weight of the vessel complemented by the keen maneuvering of the Marietta launch team recovered the vessel and it safely set sail. The yard closed in 1967.

The floodwall was built around the city following the floods of 1913 and 1937 to offer protection for the city residents and businesses. The Point Pleasant Ordnance Works, referred to as the TNT plant, had helped Point Pleasant to remain rather unscathed financially, during the Second World War, by bringing industry and jobs to the small town. The TNT plant located across 8,323 acres in Point Pleasant was a United States Army ammunition manufacturing facility. The plant produced 720,000 tons of TNT per day during the war effort from 1942-1945. All of these economic situations brought Point Pleasant into the 1950s with a positive and productive entrance. The 1950s were filled with all sorts of openings, expansions and renovations. Parades filled the streets with local schools, businesses and residents in full participation. From the relocation of Chief Cornstalk's grave to Tu-Endie-Wei to the rebuilding of the Mason County Courthouse, all venues were experiencing movement. Jack Fruth was young, but recognized the potential and need for a pharmacy in Point Pleasant. After all, this would place him back in West Virginia and close to his family. He had begun to place the stepping-stones toward his goal.

In 1951, Jack and Babs shared a first home together on West Church Street in Xenia, Ohio. Jack was still attending OSU and would graduate in June of 1951. Babs was teaching Vocational Home Economics at a consolidated school in Utica, Ohio. Their home was halfway between the schools and a compromise for the two. Money was tight. Jack had Babs write down every penny they spent for anything. It was a necessity not a preference. She recalled, "He was meticulous with his accounting skills."

Jack and Babs Fruth, Ohio State University School of Pharmacy
Graduation, June 1951

After graduation, the time had arrived for Jack to take his pharmacy board exam. The two drove from Xenia, Ohio to Morgantown, West Virginia for this all-important exam. It was a long five-hour drive in the June heat without an air-conditioned car. Upon arrival in Morgantown, Babs patiently waited while Jack endured question after question. When he finished, she was there for him and the two could relax and begin the drive home. It seemed appropriate to celebrate in some fashion. After all, this was a huge accomplishment for Jack to have had the opportunity to test for approval to become a pharmacist in 1951. It had been a long road for Jack to get to this point. It was a hot summer day; the windows were rolled down, summer's simmering heat pelted the windshield, and a Dairy Queen was on the horizon. With only twenty-five cents between them, Jack and Babs shared one ice cream cone. When asked what flavor, she paused for a moment or two. It was as though the memory flashed across her face. She said, "Well you know what? It was vanilla."

After several weeks had passed, the results were received in the mail and Jack was officially a Registered Pharmacist. He secured his first job at Gallaher Drug and worked at both the Springfield and Xenia locations. While working as a staff pharmacist for this company, he quickly realized that he wanted to own and operate his own retail pharmacy. His son John recalled:

> Dad once told me that when he put his notice in to leave Gallaher Drug they wanted him to stay. Upon receiving his letter of resignation, they told him that they would gladly give him a raise to retain him. He told them, 'no thank you.' And that if he wasn't worth more money yesterday then why would he be worth more today?

With the desire to return to West Virginia, he began planning how this dream could become a reality. He, his parents and sisters remained in close contact despite the distance between them. After much collaboration with his parents and full support from his now expectant wife, the decision was made to embark on a business endeavor in Point Pleasant, West Virginia. Many late nights and nearly every weekend were spent dreaming about, and planning this journey. He carefully and strategically placed his stepping-stones one-by-one all the way back to West Virginia. At this time, in the early 1950s, Point Pleasant was a growing and desirable place to live and work. The proximity to the river afforded much employment for the local folks, more than enough. New families arrived monthly and with that followed the need for retail goods and services. Jack knew much about many things, but he knew everything about the retail business. There were many meetings with his parents to consider the location and layout of what was soon became Fruth Pharmacy, as we know it today. Everything from fixtures to drugs had to be considered for placement and purchase.

The location of 2119 Jackson Avenue had been chosen. Jack and his father knew that the proper location was pivotal for success. Not unlike today, there was one road into Point Pleasant and one road out—Jefferson Avenue. That was where they wanted it to be. It needed to be easily accessed by those intending to stop and even more obviously visible for those not intending to do so. With every customer entering the store, there was potential for a sale. Jack knew that.

Kauffman-Lattimer (K-L) allowed Jack to order wholesale prescription drugs and other products while Columbus Showcase provided fixtures, shelving and miscellaneous hardware to display merchandise. The store was being stocked with the basics: drugs, a limited selection of sundries, a full-service soda fountain and the single most valuable commodity that Jack had to offer—supreme customer service.

With the store reaching its final stages of planning, it was time to find a home within close proximity to it. Jack knew the time that was necessary to work in order to make it a success. He was concerned that Babs was new to the area and didn't know the local folks. He wanted her to be comfortable in knowing that he was not far away. New homes were being built and rented, in Point Pleasant, as quickly as folks arrived to occupy them. Jack and Babs found a house to rent at 177 North Park Drive, in October of 1952. Their son, Mike, had been born at Greene Memorial Hospital in Xenia, Ohio on August 7, 1952—just two months before. Babs and Mike made the move first, while

Jack finished out his notice at Gallaher Drug and continued to finalize the last minute plans to open Fruth Pharmacy. Their new neighborhood of Park Drive was then referred to as Country Club Housing. This was a group of small homes built with two varying styles of floor plans, one a bit smaller than the other. The young family would not stay there long. With prospective renters outnumbering homeowners, it was a landlord's market. They had much growth and many moves to endure before they reached a final destination, both professionally and personally.

Jack's parents, Henry and Marjorie still owned and operated The Fountain in Mason, West Virginia. They had since moved from the 'big house' in Buffalo in 1947, while Jack was away at school. Union Carbide had purchased their 'big house' as their first section of property on which to build a large factory. Nothing more was ever completed by Union Carbide and several years later Toyota purchased the property. The Fruth home was torn down. Today[5], the main office for the Toyota plant rests on the exact spot where the 'big house' was situated. As a result of their home being purchased by Union Carbide, Henry and Marjorie had purchased a log cabin on a hill located behind what is now a greenhouse in the Midway area of Middleport, Ohio. They remained there for eight years. While Henry and Marjorie were helping Jack get started with the new store, they began to contemplate relocating themselves to Point Pleasant. It would be three more years before they did so.

On November 1, 1952, at 2119 Jackson Avenue Point Pleasant, West Virginia, the first Fruth Pharmacy opened its doors to the public. The only additional worker with Jack that first day was his mother, Marjorie. The two filled prescriptions, clerked and operated the soda fountain. At the end of that first

---

[5]   *Today being 2011*

day, they had taken in thirty-seven dollars. The town residents welcomed the store and a relationship had begun. It truly was a personal relationship. Jack went above and beyond to ensure his project was a success and not just for financial gain, he loved it. He gave his heart and soul to his profession; he was the heart and soul of his business, Fruth Pharmacy. He posted his name and phone number on the front door of the store, so that if there was an emergency, after normal business hours, he could be reached. If a child needed medication during the night, he gladly returned, opened the store and dispensed the needed preparation(s).

Babs recalled countless occasions when Jack was stopped and thanked by a parent for whom he had opened the pharmacy for, during the night, to provide a vaporizer or medication for their sick child. At times when folks were unable to pay, he held an account for them. He did things that were out of the ordinary, things that mattered. Such were the acts of compassion and generosity of Jack Fruth, even in the beginning, that touched the lives of so many. And he did so without ever expecting anything in return.

The summers were very hot. There was no air conditioning, no backdoor and no ventilation. Jack often worked without a t-shirt under his pressed, white dress-shirt that was accompanied by a bow tie and dark slacks. With hair thinning, an oval face and smiling from ear-to-ear, he was there. The floors were hardwood marred by the footsteps of their previous guests. It was not unusual to begin the day with the door propped open with the hope that a breeze entered. It most often did not. The air was filled with dusty smells of powder, sounds of the blender spinning sodas and the clatter of tablets hitting the pill tray. Jack was behind the pharmacy counter living his dream. It would be some time before additional employees were added. The first official employee during the initial year in business was Mildred Chapman. Eventually a high school student was hired to run the soda fountain after school when it was the busiest. The journey had begun. With the goal of leaving folks feeling better when they left the store than when they entered, Jack's journey continued. He worked seven days a week for years, later six days, and only much later five days per week. He was remembered to have said, *"The harder that I work, the luckier I get."*

Jack Fruth 1950s, Fruth Pharmacy Store #1

A Decade of
Safe Passage

*Whether you turn to the right or to the left, your ears
will hear a voice behind you, saying, "This is the
way; walk in it."* Isaiah 30:21 (NIV)

In the 1950s, Jack realized that an integral part of leaving folks
with a feel better experience was not only dispensing remedies at
the pharmacy counter but also by concocting beverages at the soda
fountain. The swivel stools and the chrome-plated countertops of
the fountain area became very inviting to customers. It was a place
to be social, feed your craving for sweets and leave feeling better
than when you arrived. Soda fountains were not a new fixture but
Jack understood their importance to the success of his store. In
1832 John Matthews of NYC and John Lippincott of Philadelphia
began manufacturing soda fountains. Other pioneering
manufacturers were Alvin Puffer, Andrew Morse, Gustavus
Dows and James Tufts. By 1891 the four largest manufacturers,
Tufts, Puffer, Lippincott and Matthews, formed the American
Soda Fountain Company. It was Jacob Baur, a pharmacist, who
began to manufacture carbon dioxide filled tanks and in doing so
introduced an entirely new interest to the beverage, carbonation.
He started the Liquid Carbonic Company in 1888 and began to
manufacture and market the Liquid Carbonic Soda Fountain in

the early 1900s. A potential soda jerk could purchase a fountain and a recipe manual from Baur and set up shop. The connection between pharmacy and the soda fountain was that people could procure a fountain drink to cure or aid some physical malady. In the early years several of the soda fountain beverages were concoctions of extracts, various drugs that were flavored and effervesced to make them palatable. Prior to 1914 basically every drug was over the counter so there were no limits as to what the druggist could add to your beverage; cocaine and caffeine were the most famous. In later years, the soda fountain beverages were just plain full of sugar and carbonation offering up mouth watering results flavored with Coca-Cola, cherry, grape, or any one of many available flavors. The soda fountain drew in considerable income, increased foot traffic and became an instant crowd pleaser. The 1950s has been referred to as the age of the soda fountain. It reached prime during that decade and began to lose popularity in the 1960s as the drinks began to be viewed as habit forming. And perhaps most wearing on the sales and popularity were the emerging fast food businesses. Slowly but readily there became other options for quenching a thirst and better yet you could get a burger and fries with it. Nevertheless, the soda fountain played an important role medicinally, socially and economically, at Fruth Pharmacy for many years. Local residents remembered the Fruth soda fountain to have served some of the best chicken salad sandwiches ever—thanks to Marjorie's keen cooking abilities.

Another important change during the 1950s was how teenagers were viewed. Prior to this decade teenagers were thought of as just children. With that mindset came the disregard for their future influences on the economy. This changed in the 1950s. Teenagers became an important tier of society. Merchants, politicians and others realized teenagers would very quickly become consumers and voters. Hence, Jack's soda fountain was not only providing a hangout for refreshments to teenagers but it was building a foundation for his business future, one that was strongly pillared with loyal consumers.

This was also a time of great affluence after the depression years. The World Wars consumerism took off in a big way and Jack had placed himself in the retail core. The realm of pharmacy practice was changing. Jack had a great grasp of understanding the discoveries that were emerging given his strong background in research and chemistry. New medicines abounded due to more available research. Prescription and non-prescription (over-the-counter) drugs were distinguished from one another for the first time in the United States as the pharmaceutical industry matured. Luis E. Miramontes invented the first oral contraceptive, the Pill. Although first tested in Puerto Rico, it's popularity quickly spread. Perhaps the most meaningful medical story to people of the time was that of Jonas Salk and his "conquest of polio." Adding to the new discoveries in the pharmaceutical field, 1956 saw the debut of the antipsychotic drug Thorazine, and tranquilizers such as Miltown and Equanil. These were joined by all sorts of breakthroughs for treatment of high blood pressure with diuretics, treatment of arthritis with cortisones, treatment of infection with antibiotics and many others. Jack was at the core for the retail pharmacy potential of all these discoveries. With his education in the medical field coupled with his retail experience he was well positioned to relay these services on to the general public. And the population in Point Pleasant, like many other small towns across the United States, was growing. It was a win-win situation, good for the merchant and good for the consumer.

The residents of Point Pleasant at this time, including Babs, liked to play cards, bridge. It is a bit of trick-taking card game using a standard deck of fifty-two playing cards. Bridge requires four players in two competing partnerships with partners sitting opposite each other around a small table. In Point Pleasant this gathering involved numerous small tables because one hundred or more people attended. They would gather at various places in town from the Parrish Hall of the Catholic Church to the old Moose building. The planning for each gathering would start early and would require: eight hostesses, a minimum of twenty-five tables, decks of cards, refreshments and the local expert baker would be commissioned to bake one of her lip-smacking cakes for the evening. It was a huge social event for ladies only.

People born in the 1950s were commonly referred to as baby boomers. After surviving the world war in the 1940s, people felt confident enough to have children. So they did. The Fruth family welcomed their fair share of baby boomers, the second of which was Joan. The labor pains began around nine o'clock that night. Henry and Marjorie were called and shortly thereafter arrived to stay with their grandson, Mike. The Lloyd-Maloney Clinic was just down the street. Doctors Lloyd and Maloney had come to Point Pleasant from Buena Vista, California to practice medicine. Point Pleasant offered that small town charm with much opportunity to prosper as new businesses opened doors and jobs prevailed. Folks moved in from all over the United States. The community offered a safe haven to raise children and the next to join the crowd, was a baby girl. The labor was very short, as Babs recalled. Their first daughter, Joan Elizabeth Fruth, was born on September 5, 1953 at 12:15 am. The first Fruth daughter was received with much love and affection. Dr. Maloney was out of town, so Dr. Lloyd delivered her. She and Mike were just thirteen months apart in age and became nearly inseparable, as the years passed.

Joan recalled:

> When I got old enough, Dad would take me along on small trips, work errands. When he bought a new store, he would come to the house gather up those who wanted to run back over and check out the new place.

I would volunteer to go. We would walk through, me on his shirttail, as he took copious notes of the future plans for each and every nook and cranny. My dad was a note writer and lots of them.

As the Fruth family grew, so did the business. Fruth pharmacy continued to expand and in 1955 relocated to 2419 Jackson Avenue (the present site of Duke's Cleaners). The store remained operational at this location for five years. Marjorie began to work in the store on a regular basis. Henry and Marjorie bought a house in Point Pleasant to join Jack and Babs. The house they purchased was on the main thoroughfare in town and just two doors up from what was then the store. It was a small house. They called it the red house because it had red siding. They only lived there for two years. After that Henry and Marjorie bought a larger, two-story home next door to that one and remained there for a few years. Later those two homes were torn down and now serve as business fronts with second story apartments on Jefferson Avenue. Their final move was into a home they built on Jefferson Avenue in 1962. This was the home Jack would walk to on his lunch break to join his mother for a bite to eat and watch their program. Henry continued to buy and sell properties along Jefferson Avenue. He had a keen mind for knowing where to invest.

On May 28, 1957, the growing Fruth family welcomed a second daughter, Carol Rhodes Fruth. Just thirteen months following Carol's birth, Lynne Morrow Fruth joined the family on June 10, 1958. With a growing business and family, Jack's journey was beginning to get even more interesting.

In 1959, Hidden Valley Country Club[6] opened to the community. Jack was instrumental in the opening of the golf course. He became an avid golfer and often played with Knox Dye,

---

[6] *At the time of this publication, Jim Capehart owns the Hidden Valley Country Club.*

the editor for the Point Pleasant Register throughout the years. The 9-hole regulation length golf course features 3,106 yards of golf from the longest tees for a par of 36, a 33.5 rating and a 106 slope. Loren Perrish designed the course. Carl Fruth owned the property and it was called the Poor Farm. It consisted of an old building situated at the top of the hill that was later torn down when the clubhouse was built. There was a pond at the top of this hill that became the number six green. Jack and the children fished there on several occasions. The club was once highly visited and provided private membership options with the availability of a sizeable swimming pool and tennis courts. The clubhouse had a sit down restaurant that served up hot dogs, burgers, sandwiches, cold drinks, ice creams and candies. There was a shower and locker facility to offer those enjoying the club the convenience of a changing area. The sports shop located inside the clubhouse offered club rental along with a small selection of golf and tennis supplies for sale. On occasion there were the availability of golf or tennis lessons for those interested.

Not only was Point Pleasant shaping and changing during the journey through the 1950s but also pharmacies were experiencing much change. During a more recent visit with Patty Wade on the God is Good local television program, Jack reflected on the changes in the practice of pharmacy. He said had this to say:

> Times have changed tremendously. There are so many more drugs and it's such an increased pace. There just is not as much time as in the past.

He explained to Patty that it always made him feel good when people returned to the pharmacy afterwards feeling better. He said:

It's a good feeling to know you had a hand in helping someone and making their lives better.

He further explained his thoughts on the acquaintances that you make during the day. He said:

We have the opportunity to leave an impact on everybody we meet during the course of our lives. It could be good. It could be bad. But we should all strive to make it a positive touching and not a negative one. At times we lose our train of thought and don't do that but we should strive to. It would be wonderful if everyone we met with or talked with during the day could walk away and say, well I am glad I had the chance to talk with you today.

Jack and Marjorie Fruth 1950s

Typical Fruth Pharmacy sale ad from the 1960s

Typical Fruth Pharmacy sale ad from the 1960s

Transitioning Through The 1960s

"A time to love, and a time to hate; a time of war, and a time of peace." Ecclesiastes 3:8 (KJV)

With a wife, four children and a growing business, Jack continued further on his journey. In 1960, a new store was constructed to accommodate the growing business at 2501 Jackson Avenue. The building expanded twice over the years and was later remodeled to include the addition of a drive-thru window for more convenient customer service. By 1960 Fruth Pharmacy had become the largest pharmacy in West Virginia, encompassing 6,000 square feet. In less than eight years Jack had risen to the top of his field as a pharmacy proprietor. He was on the right path and the next reward was another son. On January 6, 1960, the family welcomed their fifth child, John Rothgeb Fruth. Although Pleasant Valley Hospital had opened in 1959, John was the first child of a board member to have been born there.

Jack served as chairman of the board from 1960-1967 for the Green Acres Center for the mentally retarded. He was there from the beginning in support of this project, before any of the buildings were constructed. Jack got involved through his association with Dave McGinnis, who was close to the project because his daughter was in need of care. Many of the people that started Green Acres had children afflicted with mental and/ or physical challenges. The goal was to give these children, many of which grew into adults on location, a productive environment in which to live and work. Jack got busy. He and a group of local citizens worked to obtain land along Route 2 and funding to establish a center for developmentally disabled people to learn, work and live. Though other states such facilities, at that time, West Virginia did not. Originally it started with house parents assigned to chaperone the young men and women, usually local people, during their time at the facility. Later, they arranged for a bus to transport some children in for the day so they could learn and work. Official construction of Green Acres got underway in 1967. As time passed, more buildings were constructed including permanent residences.

In the beginning, the children and young adults crafted all sorts of things to sell in order to make money, from glass globes to colored rocks. They grew plants and flowers from seeds to raise money and still do today. But the most prominent service they offered to our community was the sale of bottled water. Today the facility is known as the Green Acres Regional Center Inc., in Lesage, West Virginia. It functions as a training center for people with disabilities. Among the 130 people there, a number of those are learning motor skills by bottling water in 5-gallon jugs for offices and 20-ounce bottles for the state parks. Jack always had an affinity for West Virginia State Parks and little did he know all those years ago that the cause he chose to support, with the welfare of less fortunate children in mind, would tap such success. The source of the water is a well. Director Jon Floyd said the water was named best-tasting water in the world a few years ago, garnering awards and accolades. Green Acres produces about 700,000 gallons a year, and the plant has grown dramatically during the past decade. Today Green Acres joins forces with ResCare to allow for growth and improvement. The facility serves people from Mason, Lincoln, Cabell and Wayne counties.

In 1962, Jack purchased Corrick Drug on Main Street in Point Pleasant. This pharmacy was operated as City Pharmacy for several years. His pharmacy staff originally consisted of Bill Hockenberry, R.Ph., and later included Bernie Smith, R.Ph. Though it burned to the ground in 1969, he still had the larger store in Point Pleasant. This was a huge financial loss for Jack's company. He chose not to rebuild the pharmacy but to focus his attention on the store uptown. And that he did. The pharmaceutical world continued to experience new advances in prescription drug availability. Valium was discovered in 1960 and hit the market in 1963. It rapidly became the most prescribed drug in history. It wouldn't take long before controversy and dependency followed the heavily prescribed drug. It's popularity accelerated prescription volumes. This pushed Jack's profits forward, along with the availability of more and more drugs for hypertension, arthritis and infections. With prescription volume on the rise there was also a surge of new retail products on the market in the 1960s. These were things Jack could market in his store. The first handheld calculators were available, cassette players and tapes came along as well as all sorts of gadgetry. These were just the sorts of items folks went to Fruth Pharmacy to find. From the arrival on the market of pantyhose, Polaroid film and cameras, Jack retailed it all at Fruth Pharmacy.

While Jack was working and growing his business, his family was playing and growing at home. Babs recalled the incident they now refer to as the "great escape." It was 1962 and not unusual for the children to play outside for long periods of time. They lived at 511 Chandler Drive in Point Pleasant and just a few blocks from the store. Mike was ten years old. The city was filled with homes that were full of children. So having someone to play with was never a problem. On this particular day, there were three kids from the house next door, four of the Fruth children (John was too young) and five kids from across the street; twelve total. It proved a large enough number to allow creative minds to get into mischief. It was a mid-summer's afternoon and Babs recalled looking out the window to check on the children to find that she couldn't see any of them. She listened. She couldn't hear them. That was the most unusual. She walked about outside of the house and called for them but to no avail. She couldn't go far, she had John. She called Jack at the store. She said, "Jack I need you to come home. I cannot find the children anywhere!" He found someone to watch the store and he hurried home. Where could they all have gone? Jack and Babs were beginning to panic. How could twelve children disappear without anyone seeing any unusual behavior? And they were a noisy gang—someone would have heard them if foul play had been involved. Jack began to think. Where would they be? Jack set out in the car on a different sort of journey this time. He drove slowly looking down all the city blocks and around all the buildings and houses. He couldn't see or hear them anywhere. More time passed. Babs was worried. Jack came back to the house. He and Babs asked themselves, where would they disappear to given the opportunity? What was their favorite thing to do? At the same time, they both said, "The river!" Jack took off, went down Lucas Lane, the same path he took the children on when they went fishing and found them at the river! What a relief. It took hours to find them. They didn't do that again.

Any and all opportunities to fish were fair game. It was mid May of 1964 and Babs asked Carol what she had in mind for her birthday. After all she would be turning seven years old on May 28. The answer was an easy one for Carol. She wanted nothing more than to go fishing with the entire family. It was a competitive sport for them; Jack always teased to see who could catch the most. Carol recalled, "I caught more fish that day than anyone else! It was a great day. Dad was happy when he fished."

It was not unusual for Jack to tender a helping hand to extended family members. The arrival of Babs' sister, Lynnette (Winnie), and her two daughters showed another example of Jack's gentle heart. Winnie and her family had suffered a serious hardship. When Babs heard about her sister's misfortune, she told Jack. He sent for them and offered safe harbor until things improved. While in Point Pleasant, Winnie worked as Jack's secretary. She stayed for a year and a half before moving back to Columbus, Ohio in 1965 to reunite with her husband. This was yet another example of Jack's perspicacious ability to route life's journey in a bountiful direction not only for himself but also for others.

On July 28, 1965 Jack's father, Henry Edward Fruth died after a battle with cancer. He was born, one of eleven children, February 5, 1891 in Mason, West Virginia. He had been instrumental in Jack's life. From the beginning he had taught Jack the importance of family dedication and public service through his example. Jack's dedication to his family never faltered. For years, Jack's sister, Kathryn, had worked in Charleston as a secretary. The day their father was buried, her employer unexpectedly died. Without notice or time to make alternate arrangements, she found herself without work. Jack took this opportunity and encouraged her to join him in Point Pleasant. She followed her brother's advice and made the move. She worked at Peoples Bank for several years before becoming his official secretary at Fruth Pharmacy. Her work at the store had become such a part of her life that even in her later years, she would take a restful seat in the prescription area and visit with folks for several hours at a time. She worked at Fruth Pharmacy until 2005. Kathryn passed away October 5, 2006, one year following Jack's death.

Jack was one of the founders of Peoples Bank (now known as City National Bank) located at 2212 Jackson Avenue in Point Pleasant, West Virginia. He served as one of the original members on the board of directors. He said, "This town needs a bank that will loan the working class people money." He served as chairman of the bank's executive committee from 1965-1988 when he was appointed chairman of the board. Jack served in the banking community for thirty-three years. In doing so, he facilitated as much help to the community as possible via loans granted to the local residents. The original location of the bank was on the corner of Fifth and Main Street in Point Pleasant. The bank shared residence with the Fruth Barbershop. With a few steps up, you entered the bank. With a few steps down, you entered the barbershop. A large window faced the sidewalk on Main Street; passersby could glance in to see Carl barbering on any given day. And the local children, who accompanied their dads for haircuts, could spend what seemed hours watching the fish swim about in the shop's tank.

With much commerce and traffic frequenting Main Street in Point Pleasant it should not come as a surprise that the odds of experiencing a mishap or two throughout the years increased. The Silver Bridge connected West Virginia to Ohio spanning the Ohio River. In doing so, the bridge delivered traffic to and from the upper end of Main Street in Point Pleasant. On December 15, 1976, disaster struck and resulted in not only a catastrophic tragedy but also many heartfelt losses. The unimaginable had happened. It was most likely the result of a disintegrated structure entrapped with heavy traffic flow that caused the collapse of the Silver Bridge into the Ohio River. In broad daylight on that cold day in December, thirty-seven vehicles were tossed from the failing structure. Forty-six people were dropped into the depths of the frigid, muddy river water and forty-four of them died. Two bodies were never recovered. Not many, if any other disaster affected Point Pleasant to the magnitude of the bridge falling that winter. There were all sorts of claims to fault the tragedy from the mysteries of the Mothman to the curse of Chief Cornstalk. Following months of investigation, it proved to be the result of the bridge's unusual eyebar-chain suspension (one of only three such structures in the world). The suspension simply gave way plunging victims to a tragic end. According to the National Transportation Safety Board, the eyebar-chain design was the key to its collapse. In many ways, this changed Point Pleasant forever. With the construction of the replacement bridge, The Silver Memorial Bridge, the traffic was routed around Main Street. This took a toll on the local business owners downtown, Jack Fruth included. Just as the traffic bypassed Main Street so did the consumers.

On January 3, 1969, a fire destroyed City Pharmacy on Main Street. This was more than a fork in the road along Jack's journey. It was devastating. The fire started in the apartment above the pharmacy. A lamp had fallen and caught fire on a mattress. In those days, things not only burned but also burned quickly. Someone on Main Street noticed the smoke escaping the roof's edge of the building and chaos ensued. The fire department was notified. Buildings were evacuated. Fires like these were very dangerous. As many Main Street buildings were constructed, the side of one becomes the wall of the next. Which translates to your neighbor's disaster can quickly become your misery. More and more smoke seemed to birth way from the edges of windows, seams of the roofs and the cracks around the doors. Initially folks thought it would be contained to the apartment in which it started. When the employees left the store, they did so without gathering files or money from the pharmacy. At that time, it seemed to be producing mostly smoke. With primitive means to fight the situation, the fire gained fervor. Not only did it ruin City Pharmacy but it also managed to destroy businesses on each side. Babs recalled when the children got out of school that day; they went to Kentucky Fried Chicken. With dinner in hand and as a family, they joined Jack downtown to recover what they could. They spent the entire evening there together rummaging through debris and salvaging the things that they could. With little to no insurance, this was a great financial loss for Fruth Pharmacy. There were challenges along the way, but Jack did not let them force him off track.

While transition through the 1960s was not without turbulence, it presented many new opportunities through which Jack sewed several fruitful seeds. Pleasant Valley Hospital was well on the way to delivering quality health care to the residents of Mason County and surrounding areas. Green Acres was developing into a respectable facility and helping those with special needs. And Peoples Bank was serving the local community. Although Fruth Pharmacy had taken a hit, it continued toward the next frontier, under Jack's navigation.

Fruth Pharmacy Soda Fountain 1960

The Fruth Family, 1960s, Fruth Pharmacy Soda Fountain Counter

Jackson Avenue, Point Pleasant

Jack Fruth, 1960s, Fruth Pharmacy

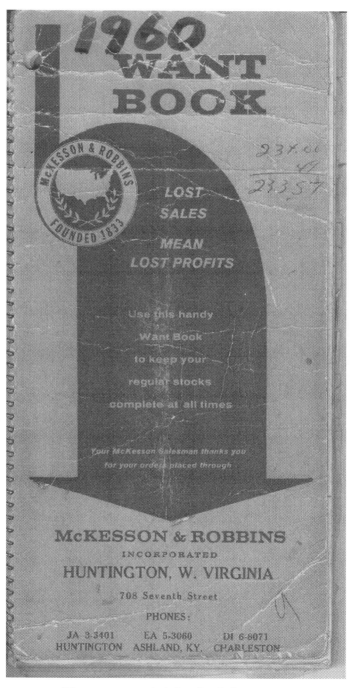

This is an example ledger book from 1960,
with handwritten daily sales totals, strategies and goals.

NATIONAL AVERAGES FOR
BUSINESS — BY MONTHS.
200,000. Goal.

1960.
1961.

16,480.97   JANUARY — 17,000   —   8% of years total
16,972.21

14,173.33   FEBRUARY — 15,000   —   7.2%
12,969.66

13,437.68   MARCH — 17,000   —   8%
17,126.42

14,318.42   APRIL — 15,000   —   7.2%
16,592.97

14,629.96   MAY — 16,000   —   7.6%
17,381.93   86,130.

13,281.62   JUNE — 16,000 96,000   —   7.6%
16,450.00

13,810.48   JULY — 15,000   —   7.2%
17,851.71

13,661.77   AUGUST — 16,000   —   7.6%
18,902.04

15,478.93   SEPTEMBER — 16,000   —   7.6%
19,347.33   (143)

14,717.71   OCTOBER — 17,000   —   8%
18,482.02

16,880.84   NOVEMBER — 16,000   —   7.6%
29,502.17

26,153.67   DECEMBER — 24,000   —   11.3%

1. GROW or Die
2. Diversify or Die
3. Progress or Perish

(1 — 197,675.07)

This is an example ledger book from 1960,
with handwritten daily sales totals, strategies and goals.

A Decade Of
Personal Hardships

"Jack Fruth was a great listener, boss and one of the greatest people I ever knew. He could take a nickel and in five-minutes make five thousand dollars from it. I miss him," Ruth Flowers.

Fruth Pharmacy operated as a sole proprietorship from 1952 through 1970 at which time it was incorporated. The necessary application procedures were completed for the process and at this time Jack learned that name "Fruth Inc." was already taken, in the state of Ohio. How could that be? The name wasn't a familiar one. Upon further investigation, it proved that Jack's great-uncle who had traveled through West Virginia all those years ago and decided to part ways with his brother had been a business owner himself. He owned and operated a hardware store in the state of Ohio. In doing so, he claimed the title, Fruth Inc., first. This was unexpected. Jack made the decision to modify his application. Why not simply use Fruth Pharmacy of Ohio, Inc.? So by including 'of Ohio', the task was a successful one. Though the Fruth brothers had parted ways on the banks of the Ohio River all those years ago, their entrepreneurial roots continued to run deep. With one great-uncle in the hardware business the vein reached to a nephew in the pharmacy business. The Fruth family represented the true spirit of private enterprise.

In 1970, Don G. Pullin, R.Ph., came to work for Fruth Pharmacy. He had been the longtime president of Corrick Drug. His employment with Fruth Pharmacy would be instrumental in the growth and development of the chain. The two men became much more than business partners. They developed a personal relationship most fitted as father and son. Mr. Fruth trusted Don and named him president of the company. The two worked closely together during those formative years. They opened store after store and made great headway toward financial success.

Although the business was on a positive footing, the personal lives of the family were not without some hardships. Carl W. Fruth died from a punctured lung injury in December of 1971, following an automobile accident. He was seventy-three years old. His sister, Helen, was a passenger in the car as well and she survived without serious harm. Nora Fruth Loomis, another sister was driving the car. Carl's death was sudden and unexpectedly left Helen living alone. Considering the two had never been separated their entire lives, his passing left her in great sadness. She was the sole beneficiary of his estate. She continued in his footsteps, managing his rental properties and working as a beautician in the barbershop. She did so and lived for many years after his death until she passed away on March 12, 1990.

Unfortunately, December brings tragedy a second time for the Fruth family. Carl's death was the first. This time it was on December 30, 1973 when the family was thrown into complete despair. Jack's sister, Henrietta, had two children, Henry and James. Henry David was the first grandson born to Henry and Marjorie Fruth. He was outgoing, handsome, do-it-all, be-it-all, and just about to graduate from Salem College, the very pride of his family. It was just after Christmas and a late night out for a few lively boys. Twenty two year old Henry was one of them.

The boys were at the traffic circle, in Point Pleasant, racing cars. The other young man he was racing, was in the lead. He turned around to see where Henry was and noticed Henry's car veered off the road, plowed through a field and then hit a tree. Having suffered severe injuries, Henry was rushed to St. Mary's Hospital and placed in intensive care. His mother never left his bedside and Jack was never far from his heartbroken sister. Visitors were limited, two at-a-time, during those long days in the ICU. Jack would join them at the hospital and remain in the waiting area, in the event he was needed or even if he was not. Days ran into evenings and then the nights came. Jack snored. Henrietta told people that, during the night, while at her son's bedside in the quiet of the hospital what she heard was her brother snoring from all the way down at the end of the hall. She knew Jack was there and it comforted her. On the home front, the entire family became available to support one another. Carol and Lynne sat with their grandmother, Marjorie, during the day. Marjorie wasn't physically able to go visit Henry or Henrietta so she wrote. She had suffered a heart attack in January of 1972. With the start of each day came a new letter. Marjorie wrote to her daughter daily to offer words of love and comfort from home. It was described as a time when they found themselves in the midst of a great catastrophe and one that ended with the worst possible outcome. Young Henry lay in a coma for twelve days until he passed away on January 10, 1974. It initially seemed the automobile accident was the cause of the injury that resulted in his death, but it was later found to be an aneurism. He had experienced headaches for some time before the accident, but a diagnosis of the cause had not been established. It remained unclear if the excitement of the automobile accident caused the aneurism to burst or if it was just the time. Lynne recalled going over to Henrietta's house weeks after Henry had passed, with Carol. The two sisters were to there to take down the Christmas tree. She recalled the tree still remained, quiet like, in their living room with all the holiday trimmings in place and several of Henry's opened presents underneath. They took it down and tucked all the decorations neatly away for Henrietta. But his gifts were still there. The girls decided to take them to his room. They opened his door and there it was, just as he left it the night of the car accident. His clothes were strewn about the furniture and floor. His shoes were by the door. They put his things away. Henry David's death was a huge hurdle to say the least. The entire family was somber and heavily weighted by the loss of their beloved Henry David.

Henrietta, in particular, suffered greatly from the bereavement of her son. They just did not know if she was going to rebound. Jack knew she needed something to throw herself into to keep her mind busy. Tabulating figures was just the task that he felt would keep her from going over the edge. It worked. Jack convinced her to take classes in tax preparation and accounting. Under his wise direction, she enrolled in the classes. Henrietta then started keeping the books for Fruth Pharmacy and became the church treasurer. Jack just had a way of shifting the direction and in doing so made everyone's journey more tolerable.

Although Marjorie was easily less than her once physically active self, following her heart attack, she still remained available for daily lunches with Jack. He would walk from the pharmacy to his mother's home on Jefferson Avenue each day. She would prepare his lunch and the two, sometimes three if Kathryn was there, would eat and then watch <u>All My Children</u> together. Yes, a soap opera and at first it may have been an innocuous pastime in order to visit with her. But Jack became hooked! So much so, that after she passed away, in 1982, he purchased his first VCR. He wanted to ensure that he could have the program taped just in the event he missed an episode. He knew all the characters and kept up with the storyline. He loved it! Kathryn had moved in with Marjorie some years earlier, so she still lived in the house;

therefore, his daily lunch date shifted to her and *they* watched <u>All My Children</u>.

As the journey through the 1970s continued, Jack together with Geary Spencer purchased White Cross Pharmacy. In 1974, this store was located at First Street and Sixth Avenue, in Huntington, West Virginia. The two men set up a corporation named S & F Pharmacy, Inc., which was fifty-percent owned by each party. It was the beginning of the Fruth Pharmacy chain of drug stores, this being store #2[7]. Jack delivered what would become his trademark beneficence to the Fruth patron: quality prescription filling, excellent customer service and a wide variety of merchandise to exceed shoppers' expectations.

With every mission there must be a little downtime in order to maintain balance. To consider Jack had spare time with all of these things going on is unimaginable but he did set a little time aside on Friday nights for poker. He loved to play cards. He and several of his friends including Dr. Boonsue, Dr. Choi, Sammy Roush (his very good friend), and Mr. Green enjoyed the opportunity to relax at the end of the workweek. Dr. Boonsue's house was the most regular spot they played. They met between six and seven in the evening and the games continued many times into the wee hours of the morning. They played for money. Babs recalled that Jack kept a little notebook reflecting his winnings and less often losses. He enjoyed the playful competition.

As the business was growing and the boys were playing poker on Friday nights, the journey continued. In 1975, the West Virginia Pharmacist's Association presented Jack with the Bowl of Hygeia Award for Community Service. The bowl of Hygeia is a community service award started in 1958 by E. Claiborne Robins, then president of A.H. Robins Co., as an acknowledgment of services rendered by selected pharmacists. These men and women

---

[7] *In consideration of the date on which this book was written, store #2 operates at 125 Seventh Avenue in Huntington, West Virginia.*

reflect an outstanding record of community service and leadership in the field of pharmacy. Hygeia, the daughter of Aesculapius and the goddess of health, is typically depicted with a serpent around her arm and a bowl in her hand because she tended to the temples containing these snakes. We have since separated the serpent and the bowl from Hygeia, and this has become the internationally recognized symbol of pharmacy. Now the bowl represents a medicinal potion, and the snake represents healing. Healing through the medicine is precisely why pharmacy has adopted the Bowl of Hygeia symbol. The American Pharmacy Association adopted the Bowl of Hygeia in 1964 as the representative symbol of the pharmacy profession.

As Jack continued to validate his professional talents, his business was taking off as a result. In 1976, Fruth Pharmacy added a third store[8] and this one was located Gallipolis, Ohio. This pharmacy was opened as a fifty-percent partnership between Jack and Don Pullin. With Don as part owner, he also worked in the store as the pharmacist-in-charge. The two men became closer and closer and as a result the business grew and grew. The gift department within the company's stores grew to stand-alone departments generating much revenue for the company. However, the pharmacy sales still provided the strength to push the financial growth forward. The men knew how to sell customer service. The residents of the communities had the option of shopping at several other places for prescription and gift needs but the customer service at Fruth Pharmacy was unmatched anywhere. Mr. Fruth decided to offer all sorts of additional service to his customers such as: utility bill collections, money orders, lottery tickets, key cutting services, package mailings, film developing and just about anything a consumer may have needed. Holiday revenues began to sky rocket from the seasonal merchandise and candy sales.

---

[8]   *As of the date on which this book was written, store #3 operates at 2991 State Route 160 in Gallipolis, Ohio.*

Store aisles were bustling with shoppers, the pharmacy was filling record numbers of prescriptions and Mr. Fruth was planning his next strategy for continued growth.

1976, Fruth Pharmacy #3, Gallipolis, Ohio

Under the establishment of another corporation, a fourth Fruth Pharmacy[9] was opened in 1979, Fruth Pharmacy of Wellston, Inc. This one was with Mike Fruth owning forty-percent, Jack, Geary Spencer, and Don Pullin each owning twenty-percent. Upon opening store #4, Mike Fruth was pharmacist-in-charge and store manager. Again the men got busy and stocked the store from floor to ceiling. Jack was a master at merchandising. In many ways, the 1970s were the start of the electronics and digital revolution with the invention of transistors and integrated circuits from the previous decade. Inventive companies now found ways to use the technology that caused the phenomenal growth in smaller more powerful and less expensive products ranging from calculators to

---

[9]   *In consideration of the date on which this book was written, store #4 operates at 120 West Second Street in Wellston, Ohio.*

televisions. Though Fruth Pharmacy didn't sell televisions, they did sell their fair share of calculators and digital alarm clocks. As the new merchandise arrived and filled the stockroom, the others followed Jack's example and before they knew it, not a bare space was apparent on any wall and there was just enough room to pass in the aisles. Another Fruth Pharmacy had opened for business.

This is an example ledger book from 1979,
with handwritten daily sales totals.

SALES

1972		1973
116,568.82	JAN.	115,929.74
120,743.43	Feb.	122,111.03
133,857.36	MAR.	136,716.07
127,013.74	APR.	129,030.80
130,088.15	MAY.	148,009.75
127,911.25	JUNE.	137,820.93
139,670.25	JULY	154,605.13
131,447.66	AUG.	141,948.81
124,853.69	SEPT.	137,439.18
128,208.17	OCT.	148,496.29
137,564.76	NOV	159,423.08
244,876.77	DEC.	287,137.03
1,662,304.05	TOTAL	1,823,587.84

This is an example ledger book from the 1970s
with handwritten daily sales totals.

A Decade Of Positive Traction

"Jack Fruth was a man of his word. You didn't have to worry about putting his promise to you in writing. When he told you that he would do something, he did it," Bob Pegg, R.Ph.

To say that the 1980s brought a growth spurt for Fruth Pharmacy is an understatement. Sit back, buckle-up and enjoy the ride. In May of 1982, Fruth Pharmacy opened a fifth store[10], in Milton, West Virginia. This one would be under the management of the pharmacist-in-charge, Charles "Laddie" Burdette. Laddie had been personally hired by Mr. Fruth in 1976 to work summers at the Point Pleasant store while he completed his pharmacy studies at West Virginia University. After which Laddie was transferred to the Route 160 store in Gallipolis, Ohio where he completed his pharmacy internship under the guidance of Don Pullin, R.Ph. Shortly thereafter, Laddie not only became the store manager and pharmacist-in-charge at the Milton location, but the owner of fifty-percent of the pharmacy. The remaining fifty-percent of ownership was equally shared by Jack, Mike Fruth and Don

---

[10]   *In consideration of the date on which this book was written, store #5 operates at 16 Perry Morris Square in Milton, West Virginia.*

Pullin. Despite a small fire that delayed the grand opening of the store for two weeks, the Milton store proved to be a pivotal point of revenue for the chain.

With the business taking off at a more accelerated pace than anticipated, Jack was hit with a hard halt. On September 8, 1982, his mother, Mrs. Marjorie M. Fruth, 85 years old, died on a Wednesday evening at the Holzer Medical Center. She was born July 25, 1897, in Gallipolis, Ohio, to the late William and Parsada Harris Rothgeb. She was a member of the Trinity United Methodist Church, the Martha Circle of United Methodist Women, the Point Pleasant Chapter No. 75 Order of Eastern Star, the Past Matron's Club and the Point Pleasant Women's Club. She was a respected member of the community, a loving mother, sister, grandmother and great-grandmother. This was a great loss for the family. She was Jack's number one supporter and had been all his life.

He turned his focus once again to the heart of his business. By the end of 1982 the chain, for the first time, was posting one million dollars in revenues each month. Jack was picking up speed. His company joined the Associated Chain Drug Stores, a group founded in 1926 to help drug stores combine their buying power as well as other services. Jack was a strong advocate for fair business for all. He was quoted to have said:

> It used to be that two chains in the same market wouldn't speak to each other. Now we are anxious to work together, so we all have a chance at the business. The feeling is no longer that as drug chains we are competitors. Our competitors are the deep discounters, the combos, the hypermarkets, the HMOs and mail order. If mail order or a K-Mart takes away business, we all suffer.

In 1983, Jack opened a sixth store[11] in Middleport, Ohio under the ownership of Fruth Pharmacy of Ohio, Inc. Store #6 was later moved to Pomeroy, Ohio in order to better service the community. The existing pharmacy was in an old grocery store and the physical structure of the building had become dilapidated over the years. Parking was limited and the addition of a drive-thru was not an option. After much thought and consideration of new placement, the store was relocated up river to Pomeroy, Ohio. Though only a few miles from the original store, the new location proved to be most successful. It would be 2008 before a new bridge, The Bridge of Honor, was constructed to span the Ohio River joining Pomeroy, Ohio to Mason, West Virginia. The move from Middleport to Pomeroy positioned the store in perfect proximity to the new bridge. Now local customers could not only cross the river with safe passage to reach the store but also shop in a modern facility with ample parking.

As the growth spurt of the 1980s continued, two more Fruth Pharmacy's opened for business and Jack's journey continued to be a blessed one. In 1984, Fruth Pharmacy opened store #7[12] in Nitro, West Virginia. The second pharmacy to open in 1984 was store #8[13] in Proctorville, Ohio. As did several others, this pharmacy opened as part of the S & F Pharmacy, Inc. Though later in years store #8 was relocated up the street just a short distance from the original one, construction at the new location proved to be a beneficial investment.

---

[11] *In consideration of the date on which this book was written, store #6 operates at 706 West Main Street in Pomeroy, Ohio.*

[12] *In consideration of the date on which this book was written, store #7 operates at 106 Twenty-first Street in Nitro, West Virginia.*

[13] *In consideration of the date on which this book was written, store #8 operates at 259 State Street in Proctorville, Ohio.*

The Synercom Pharmacy System was introduced to Fruth Pharmacy in the 1980s. Synercom is a prescription processing software system. It offered flexibility and control to pharmacy management. It offered the ability to centrally manage receivables for third party (insurance) claims and patient charges from a corporate office. As prescription volumes continued to grow (as they were with Fruth Pharmacy), speed and efficiency became much more important and this system had operations for: disease management, automated dispensing system interfaces, workflow management and integrated voice response systems (IVR touch-tone refills). It also offered management tools for financial reports and file maintenance functions from a single location and inventory management. It was a sophisticated system for the times. Jack had entered the pharmacy profession thirty years earlier when most transactions for prescriptions were done on a cash basis and patients' profiles were recorded on cards and filed alphabetically. Labels were hand-typed and carefully placed on vials. But he was not afraid of modernization to better the flow of his business. All of the Fruth stores were connected to this new system and as a result files were updated on a nightly basis, reports were run which helped management better determine what to carry and what price changes needed to be made. The typewriter was put to rest. It was saved though for the times the computer system would crash and it did.

In 1986, Fruth Pharmacy opened a ninth store[14]. This one is rather off the beaten path but that was not unusual for Jack to place a store in that type of location. He had a keen insight about marketing his stores. He was in tune to the rural areas and knew those customers needed quality services as well. Unlike the bigger stores that were beginning to emerge, Fruth continued to offer supreme customer service. Often having five or six associates

---

[14]   *In consideration of the date on which this book was written, store #9 operates at 8972 United Lane in Athens, Ohio.*

available on the sales floor to assist customers. Not to say the challenges were not there. They were. Many local jobs continued to disappear, which resulted in folks moving to new places or just not having enough money to shop as they once did. The profit margins got tighter due to more competition. Those tactics of offering supreme customer service and stocking interesting merchandise were holding strong. The company held it's own and continued forward.

As the 1980s were winding down, not slowing down, the giving nature of Jack's journey continued receiving as well. When Jack was awarded a Master's Degree in Public Service from the University of Rio Grande in 1986, he had this to say:

> President Dorsey, distinguished guests, faculty, graduates and guests: Receiving this honorary degree today is the greatest honor I have ever received. I want to share some of the reasons why this means so much to me. But first I would like to thank some of those who made it possible. I give thanks to God for watching over my family and me and for providing me the opportunities I have had in my life.
>
> I thank my mother, father and three sisters for their guidance, support and love. I thank President Dorsey, all of the board of trustee members, the faculty and students of the great university for their support and friendship during my two-year presidency and all the years that I have had the pleasure of working with you. Thanks to everybody who has contributed to making this honor possible.
>
> About fifty years ago, the greatest event of my life took place. It was the day that I met a pretty little girl from South Charleston, Ohio. After about two years of super salesmanship, I convinced her to become my

wife. Together we produced five children and eight grandchildren. My wife devoted her entire life to them and deserves all of the credit for their achievements. Every one of them has supported me wholeheartedly in all of my endeavors. I am forever indebted to them for that. I would like to ask them to all stand up and be recognized as well as my sister and brother-in-law. Thanks go to each of you.

Doctor of Pubic Service, wow! What a title; what an honor! This symbolizes what my entire working life has been because my whole life has been involved in serving the public and every day of it has been a joy. Of course, some days were trying and frustrating, at the time, but in many cases those are the days of which you have the fondest memories.

In earlier days, we were often called out in the middle of the night to fill a prescription or get an emergency need for a customer. We even posted our pharmacist's home phone number on the front door of the pharmacy. We put R.Ph. behind our names in the phone directory to make it easy for our customers to reach us.

I still encounter people occasionally who say, "I remember when you came to the store after closing hours and filled my prescription or got me a vaporizer when my baby had the croup." What a pleasure when someone remembers a service you provided or remembered a problem and you gave him or her advice and it worked. I don't accept praise or complements very graciously because I never know how to respond but it sure makes me feel good. One of the greatest satisfactions in life is helping someone.

One of my ambitions in life has always been to try to make a difference, to try to leave things a little better and to enjoy life as I did it.

When I completed my term as president of the university board of trustees, a lovely young lady, Carol Wedge, complimented me by saying that she appreciated that I tried to bring a little humor into a serious matter—probably the crummy jokes that I told occasionally. Life is serious but it still helps to laugh at ourselves once and awhile.

This is why I feel so honored to receive this degree. To me it says you have done an outstanding job in servicing the public. There are some less significant reasons I enjoy receiving this degree such as: about forty some years ago I began receiving mail from Greenbrier Military Alumni Association and it was always addressed to Dr. Jack E. Fruth. I don't know where they picked that up. I always intended to write and tell them that they were incorrect but vanity probably kept me from doing that. Now, I won't have to.

Also in the early years of my practice, it was common for many patients to call their pharmacists "Doc." I remember particularly an elderly schoolteacher in Mason County who always called me doctor.

I love receiving this degree. I love having the title of doctor. But I don't want to be a doctor to any of you. I just want each of you to continue being my friend.

In 1987, Fruth Pharmacy opened a tenth store[15] in Hurricane, West Virginia. And in October of 1987, a thirteen thousand square

---

[15]   *In consideration of the date on which this book was written, store #10 operates at 3109 Teays Valley Road in Hurricane, West Virginia.*

foot building became the Fruth corporate offices and warehouse on Route 62 in Point Pleasant, West Virginia.

The journey through the 1980s continued to be a bountiful one and in 1988, another Fruth Pharmacy opened. The eleventh store[16] opened and is referred to as the Camden Road store. In addition to the opening of Fruth Pharmacy #11, the twelfth store[17] celebrated it's opening during the same year. Store #12 is referred to as the Roby Road store.

Fruth Pharmacy expanded yet again, in 1989, to open a thirteenth store[18] in an area well positioned with busy traffic and neighboring commerce. As a matter of fact, it is the only pharmacy in town. This Fruth Pharmacy began with a unique footprint. Though the largest portion of the store was designated as a Fruth Pharmacy, a smaller portion was sectioned off and subleased. The first tenant to share floor space was a video rental business and then later Fox's Pizza. As of late, the store was remodeled due to an expansion of the pharmacy department to accommodate a drive-thru and a patient counseling area.

By the close of the 1980s, Jack was traveling at full throttle. The chain had grown to thirteen pharmacies, a corporate office and a warehouse. His humble dream of servicing the local communities was majestically flying high in the sky.

---

[16] *In consideration of the date on which this book was written, store #11 operates at 425 Camden Road in Huntington, West Virginia.*

[17] *In consideration of the date on which this book was written, store #12 operates at 1419 US Route 60 East (Roby Road) in Huntington, West Virginia.*

[18] *In consideration of the date on which this book was written, store #13 operates at 3504 Winfield Road in Winfield, West Virginia.*

An Outpouring Of
Community Encouragement

The LORD said, "*Go out and stand on the
mountain in the presence of the LORD, for the
LORD is about to pass by.*" After the earthquake
came a fire, but the LORD was not in the fire.
And after the fire came a gentle whisper. 1Kings
19:11-12 (NIV)

Following the 1980s would be an incredible task considering the
accelerated growth that Fruth Pharmacy experienced; however,
by way of acquisitioning existing pharmacies and the opening of
additional stores, we enter this decade trailing a burning wick. In
February of 1990, Fruth Pharmacy opened a fourteenth store[19].
This pharmacy is positioned in a previous Kroger location, as are
many Fruth storefronts. At the time this was the largest Fruth
pharmacy and had the most expansive magazine selection in the
State of West Virginia. This store is currently a strong merchant
in the city of Charleston and continues the Fruth tradition of
supreme customer service. It was not uncommon for Jack to make
the decision to purchase neighboring pharmacies in an effort to
solidify his business footing. Many times the contents of these

---

[19]   *In consideration of the date on which this book was written, store #14 operates
at 864 Oakwood Road in Charleston, West Virginia.*

stores were either combined with existing Fruth merchandise or sold at a reduced price. Miller Drug in Hurricane, West Virginia and The Prescription Shoppe in Athens, Ohio are two examples of such acquisitions. Store fourteen, in addition to store seventeen in Mineral Wells and store one in Point Pleasant service the prescription needs of the regional jails and juvenile centers in West Virginia.

As business continued on a positive track through the 1990s, Jack's personal life did the same. Jack and Babs celebrated their 40th wedding anniversary on December 30, 1990. In celebration of their love, Jack arranged for them to again watch *The Red Shoes*, which was the movie they watched while on their first date. In the movie, a young ballet dancer is torn between the man she loves and her pursuit to become a prima ballerina. Babs laughed and recalled that Jack said, "In retrospect it just wasn't that great of a movie. It seemed so much better forty years ago." To celebrate his love for Babs and in honor of their fortieth year together as husband and wife, he presented her with a ruby ring and earrings. The family gathered and enjoyed as Jack and Babs celebrated their anniversary with the movie, dancing, food and refreshments.

Back on the professional forefront, in 1990, Jack was awarded the Mason County Area Chamber of Commerce Community Service Award. His years of service with the chamber were another example of his involvement with Mason County.

In 1991 Fruth Pharmacy opened a fifteenth store[20] in Belpre, Ohio. This store was later replaced with a new building in September of 2000.

In 1992, Don Pullin became president of Fruth Pharmacy. After years of personal friendship and professional partnership, Jack trusted Don to have this position. The business continued to grow. During the year of 1992, Fruth Pharmacy opened a

---

[20] *In consideration of the date on which this book was written, store #15 operates at 1401 Washington Boulevard in Belpre, Ohio.*

store[21] in Waverly, Ohio to bring the total to sixteen. This store had an interesting beginning. It opened following the buyout of Kegley's Drug Store. Success began early with the Waverly Fruth. A large number of the employees came with the business. As a matter of fact, this store retains the largest number of those faithful employees today, years later. The first week it opened, it was number one in sales for the entire chain! The Waverly Fruth prevails as one of the strongest and most loyally staffed stores.

The growth spurt of the 1980s had brought much opportunity for the 1990s. During 1992 the beginning of direct importing started for Fruth Pharmacy. Don Pullin and Mike Fruth made their first visit to the orient by visiting Hong Kong. Fruth Pharmacy had now branched out to purchase merchandise direct from the manufacturer. Another turning point for Jack in 1992 was the decision to give up filling prescriptions at the age of sixty-five. Though he remained a druggist at heart, he chose to focus on overseeing his company. At that time, Fruth Pharmacy employed four hundred plus people from small towns across West Virginia and Ohio. In an article from the Point Pleasant Register, Jack was noted to have said, "*The small towns appreciate you a lot more. It's a big event when you open there.*" He found reward in knowing folks' names and being able to enjoy their patronage to Fruth Pharmacy from a pharmacist's perspective for years. He said, "*I'll miss that interplay more than anything else. You get a certain amount of satisfaction from that.*" He interacted with everyone. Having enjoyed doing most all things in his stores, he also added, "*I used to say there wasn't anything I couldn't do in the store, including sweep the floors.*" With plenty of well-set employees to continue his tradition, Jack retired from his role as pharmacist and enjoyed the new direction of his journey.

---

[21]   *In consideration of the date on which this book was written, store #16 operates at 101 James Road in Waverly, Ohio.*

Jack was awarded the Chain Drug Marketing Association (CDMA) Hall of Fame Award in 1992. CDMA was founded in 1926 by a group of chain drug owners with the ambition of forming a group whose sole purpose was supporting the owners' marketing and merchandising efforts. By this time, Jack had become well known for his merchandising skills beyond Fruth Pharmacy. CDMA has evolved in many ways since those early days. After 68 years of being headquartered in New York City, the association moved to a larger facility and distribution center in Novi, Michigan in June of 1997. Today, CDMA is a vibrant and growing Association, despite consolidation of the chain drug industry. Over 100 regional drug chains, independent pharmacies, regional drug wholesalers, specialty distributors and buying groups, own the association. It helps suppliers communicate with members through trade shows and extensive marketing programs. They differentiate themselves by supporting suppliers' sales teams 52 weeks a year, offering centralized billing, and host the Annual Education and Trade Expo for networking and relationship building. Joining its hall of fame was just another acknowledgement that Jack had earned the respect and fellowship of colleagues across the United States.

In 1993, a seventeenth Fruth Pharmacy[22] opened in Mineral Wells, West Virginia. On the grand-opening day there was a huge snowstorm. On his way to the store Laddie Burdette got stuck in a snow bank on Leon Baden Road. That didn't deter the business as usual procedures for Fruth Pharmacy. Despite the obstacles of that day, damages to the awning from the heavy snow and traveling hindrances, Fruth Pharmacy opened for business as usual.

As the early 1990s were continuing, each year marked a busy, productive and advancing mile along Jack's journey. He

---

[22]   *In consideration of the date on which this book was written, store #17 operates at Route 4, Box 681 in Mineral Wells, West Virginia.*

was awarded the Distinguished Alumni Award by Ohio State University, College of Pharmacy. Recipients of this award must have a professional degree such as a Bachelor of Science, Masters of Science or PharmD from the Ohio State University College of Pharmacy. The recipients of the award must have made distinguished contributions in the field of public health and public service as well as performed outstanding activities in the interest of the college and its students. Lastly, the recipient must have an outstanding record in the profession of pharmacy. Jack graciously accepted this prestigious award in 1993.

With Don Pullin, in a higher position to carry more responsibility, Jack began to take a little more time away from the business and to enjoy his family. In 1993, the family made the decision to purchase a thirty-acre property in Oak Hill, Ohio on Jackson Lake. Babs was primarily responsible for the purchase of this family getaway. Jack had given her the duty of making the final decision to buy the property. She not only handled the purchase but also the responsibility of making the necessary arrangements to meet the demands of ownership. There were repairs to be made and maintenance to be performed. She undertook the project and developed the family retreat into what it is today. There were two rustic cabins on the property, one for Babs and one for Joan, each within walking distance of the other. The cabins were in need of much repair from new wiring to additional construction. One day while the cabins were undergoing renovation, they walked down a wooded path on the property. They reached a point where there was once a dock. They heard a loud splash! And then they heard another splash and another splash. It was then when they discovered what caused the entire ruckus. Beavers were hitting the water off the edge of the old dock. They appropriately named the property "Beaver Point." Most recently, Joan has transformed her once cabin into a large, beautifully handcrafted home. She resides there with her fiancé Greg, along with three horses, eleven dogs and five cats. The Fruth family still visits Beaver Point as often as time permits and everyone shared a memorable story about a time they spent there with Jack. These sequences of events proved that Babs had the right idea when selecting their special retreat.

While Jack was enjoying more and more family time, the business continued to expand. In 1994, Fruth Pharmacy opened the eighteenth store[23] in Spencer, West Virginia.

In 1995, Jack was awarded the James H. Beal Award by the West Virginia Pharmacist's Association. This is the highest award granted by the West Virginia Pharmaceutical Association for outstanding service in the field of pharmacy. In this same year, he also became a member of the Who's Who in West Virginia Business. This award is based on nomination. The recipient is proven to be one of the most superior and astute business owners in the state of West Virginia. With Jack's longevity in business with Fruth Pharmacy and expansive growth, he was welcomed via nomination to join the ranks of the best and brightest West Virginians.

The Marshall University Foundation, Inc., became the recipient of a funding scholarship founded by Jack Fruth. In 1995, Dr. Carolyn Hunter, Marshall University Associate Vice President for Institutional Advancement, accepted a ten thousand dollar check on behalf of Fruth Pharmacy. Don Pullin, then president of Fruth Pharmacy, along with Jack Fruth, then chairman and chief executive officer, presented the check. Don Pullin said, "The proceeds from the Fruth Golf Tournament will be added to the fund each year. One award will be made annually to cover educational expenses for one academic year."

While enjoying the fruits of his professional labors, as award after award graced the walls of the corporate office and scholarship

---

[23]   *In consideration of the date on which this book was written, store #18 operates at 211 Bowman Street in Spencer, West Virginia.*

funds were established, in 1996, Jack purchased a bass boat. Fishing *was* his favorite hobby. With Fruth Pharmacy running smoothly, Jack would depart to Beaver Point with his family more and more. They would pack up a few things on Fridays and stay until Sunday. Joan was already there so the getaways quickly turned into family retreats, which was just the intention Babs had for the property. She recalled Jack's dislike for blue jeans and reflected on the time she had purchased him some *casual slacks* to wear for these trips to the cabin. Babs explained how he was always ruining his along the water's edge while fishing. He asked her, "Are these blue jeans, Babs?" She said, "No, honey, they are denim." She recalled that he didn't figure it out because he was colorblind. For years, the family had taken one vacation per year to a state park in West Virginia. They stayed in a cabin, swam in lakes, fished and hiked the nature trails while Babs cooked the meals. Perhaps at that time, it was the only vacation they could afford. But over the years it had become the vacation they most enjoyed. Beaver Point had all the amenities they needed and the fellowship of their family was what they wanted.

In 1996, Fruth Pharmacy expanded yet again to open two more stores. The nineteenth Fruth Pharmacy[24] opened in Ripley, West Virginia. Store #19 was unique because it was the first store to incorporate a drive-thru with the initial construction. Other stores were later retrofitted with drive-thru windows but this was the first to have one configured into the original blueprint. The twentieth store[25] for Fruth Pharmacy and the second store that opened during 1996 was in Eleanor, West Virginia. As December advanced and 1996 neared an end, the circumstance of the holiday rush was underway. The stores were fully stocked with Christmas

---

[24] *In consideration of the date on which this book was written, store #19 operates at 509 South Church Street in Ripley, West Virginia.*

[25] *In consideration of the date on which this book was written, store #20 operates at 501 Roosevelt Boulevard in Eleanor, West Virginia.*

candies, gift items and seasonal necessities. This was the time of year when the corporate warehouse became a convergence of activity. Truckloads of merchandise arrived on a daily basis and were redirected for display in one of the twenty Fruth Pharmacy locations. In years past, the Fruth family had experienced misfortunes with Carl's death in 1971 and Henry David's car accident in 1973. But the tragedy they endured this December not only involved family but also employees, the community and their business. A fire destroyed the Fruth Pharmacy warehouse and corporate offices on December 3, 1996.

Daughter Carol recalls the fire:

> I was at the warehouse working. It was early December. Joan and Mike were there, too. We were writing the invoices and packing the merchandise for shipment to each of the stores. Suddenly Mike shouted, 'TURN IT OFF!' I looked up and there were flames shooting out of the heater that hung from the ceiling. It only took what seemed like a moment for the flames to reach the tall, metal shelves that were full of merchandise, paper products (toilet tissue and paper towels). The merchandise had begun to burn. I yelled to Joan, 'DIAL 911!' Mike ran to get the rolling ladder and a fire extinguisher. Joan and I ran to get fire extinguishers. We had just had the fire-safety course the week before. Frantically, we handed Mike all the fire extinguishers that we could retrieve. With the exhaustion of the last one, the fire was still blazing with flames all over the place. It was spreading much more quickly than we could put it out. At the end of the metal shelving were two more skids that were twenty feet tall apiece and loaded with Valentine's Day merchandise. There was no end in sight. Smoke was filling the area so much

so that visibility was becoming difficult. Our eyes were burning. The overhead lights started popping, with glass blowing in every direction. Then the skids became engulfed in flames and went up in a blaze of fire. When that happened, a rush of hot air blew away from the skids and toward our bodies forcing us toward the side door. Finally, we ran outside. Mike's car was parked near the warehouse. He did not have his keys. They were left behind, inside. We stood outside the warehouse feeling helpless, overwhelmed, and in shock at what had just happened. It seemed to take forever for help to appear. The three of us waited. The fire department arrived. Now they needed a water supply to handle such a big fire. They considered pumping water from the resort pool next door to the warehouse. There was no pressure. They brought in pumper trucks. All the while, we stood there and watched it burn. Mike's car was pulled away from the warehouse with the Jaws of Life when his lights started melting. It took one-half hour for the water to hit the flames. It was too late. We were worried about our dad. What would he say? How would he react? Mother and Dad arrived. Mother was supportive and Dad handled it gracefully. Dad had watched City Pharmacy burn to the ground in previous years, so he had endured a fire. We all gathered together and sat in Dad's car. Dad said, 'As long as you kids are safe, that is all that matters.' He was like that and always knew what we needed to hear. We not only smelled smoke for what seemed like forever but also *we* even smelled like smoke. We went back to Mother and Dad's house. My son was two years old at the time. I was glad to see him. Later, I talked to the fire marshal and gave him all the information that I had about the disaster. The heater was the cause. We were very fortunate to have survived that day, very blessed to have survived that disaster. You see as kids, we grew up in an assembly line sort of fashion. If we made cinnamon toast, then each kid had a duty. John got out the bread. Joan, Lynne, or myself would apply the butter and cinnamon. And Mike would operate the oven. This day, we worked in an assembly line fashion handing fire extinguishers, one after the other, to Mike as he fought the fire. We were in a line, just like Mother and Dad taught us. That day, our brother, Mike, saved us. He really did. Mike first saw the fire, fought it, as we helped and knew when to get us out.

Though fire departments from Point Pleasant, Mason, New Haven and Flatrock, West Virginia as well as Middleport and Pomeroy, Ohio were on the frontlines, they were unable to contain the fire's destruction. It burned steadily for hours. The warehouse not only contained large quantities of paper products but also flammable materials such as: propane tanks, insecticides, hairspray and kerosene. The Leon, West Virginia fire department came forward to offer assistance and did so by setting up in Point Pleasant. They were on duty to cover any other emergencies that might have arisen while the Point Pleasant Fire Department was in full force fighting the warehouse fire. With the persistent work of the fire fighters, the company's main computer systems and important files were saved. These things were taken to the nearby National Guard armory for safe storage. The fire fighters worked tirelessly on the blaze. Some were overcome by smoke, heat and exhaustion. Although no serious injuries were caused by the blaze, emergency and medical technicians were busy tending to those in need of resuscitative care.

There was an outpouring of community encouragement. From local folks offering support to Rite Aid wanting to know if Jack would sell, the telephone calls were coming in from all directions. Much of the goodwill Jack had so freely shared along his journey was coming back around in full circle. Jack stepped up and handled the situation with care and professionalism. His company was in good hands, his own. A temporary warehouse was in operation the next day in Oak Hill, Ohio and thirty days later in Gallipolis, Ohio. The corporate officials worked out of their automobiles and out of temporary offices offered by neighbors in the city of Point Pleasant. Pharmacy administrative and information services were temporarily located at store #1 in Point Pleasant. Day-after-day, goodhearted townsfolk prepared breakfasts and lunches and sent them to the employees. Of particular merit and most remarkable, was the fact that Jack made immediate positions for all his corporate and warehouse employees. Not one Fruth Pharmacy employee missed a day of work without pay as a result of layoffs that could have occurred due to the fire. Jack embraced this unforeseen detour and proved his loyalty to them.

Investigators from the State Fire Marshall's office searched for a cause of the massive fire that caused such a huge destruction to the warehouse and found nothing of a suspicious nature. The losses exceeded two million dollars for Fruth Pharmacy. With insurance to cover the majority of the damages, there remained a substantial financial loss for the company. Under Jack's guidance, they were able to overcome.

Against what some folks may have considered impossible odds following the recent warehouse fire, the twenty-first Fruth Pharmacy[26] opened in 1997. This had already been in the planning stages for sometime, so Don and Laddie continued forward and

---

[26]   *In consideration of the date on which this book was written, store #21 operates at 204 Second Avenue in Gallipolis, Ohio.*

met the grand opening deadline for the twenty-first store. This pharmacy was within walking distance of a grocery store, as were several of the Fruth Pharmacy locations. Folks could easily drop off prescriptions for filling while getting their grocery shopping done. Jack was a master at knowing how to serve the customer with the utmost convenience. Although there was a competitor pharmacy just a block down the street, Fruth prevailed to remain the only one. With the competitor closing their doors, store #21 became busier and busier and quickly established a strong footing on the retail prescription front. Premium retail service including not only prescription filling but also balloon deliveries, a large selection of primitive giftware, free gift wrapping, greeting cards, seasonal merchandise and weekly sale ad merchandise secured Fruth Pharmacy, in the community, as a much needed shopping stop.

To say the least, the fall of 1997 was busy. Several months after the fire, not only did Fruth open the twenty-first store but also the corporate offices were reopened with improvements made including a large meeting and training center and a separate corporate conference room. In addition, a thirty thousand square foot distribution center/warehouse was also opened with the capacity for future growth. Jack's journey was again transitioning through another decade. His travels would not be complete though without him taking a moment to thank the wonderful people of Point Pleasant and Mason County for their outreaching support during the tragedy of the warehouse fire. He held an open house at the corporate warehouse and served food and refreshments. Folks stopped in, shared stories and fellowshipped with the man they had all grown to love and respect. A man of such giving nature and kind intentions toward others, often them, was the center of the celebration.

Although sales for the fiscal year of 1997 were up nine percent to sixty million dollars, March of 1998 brought costly damages to

Fruth Pharmacy. Having just recovered from the fire damages of the previous year, a levy had broken in Waverly, Ohio. The flood resulted in not only eighteen inches of water filling the store but also severe flooding to the Waverly storage facility. As Jack had so many times before taught by example, under the leadership of the corporate office personnel, appropriate measures were quickly taken to meet the needs of the customers. Although the store was closed for one day, despite the severe damages, Fruth Pharmacy was quickly reopened to serve customers.

With the damages from the fire and flood closely in the rear view mirror, the decision was made to focus attention on the internal growth of the business versus meeting the goal of opening more stores at this time. The POS system was put in place. POS is a point of sale program that allows the retailer to track usage, monitor changes in unit dollar cost, calculate when you need to reorder, and analyze inventory levels on an item-by-item basis. The system records each sale when it happens, so your inventory records are always up-to-date. It benefited Fruth Pharmacy by allowing them to run reports based on this information and make better decisions about ordering and merchandising. Fruth Pharmacy began to analyze each store's inventory. Cosmetic products were deemphasized to one-fourth of their previous floor space while bath and body products were added in large quantities. The stores added specialty food products, such as, sugar-free candies and name-brand foods and snacks. Sales for the fiscal year of 1998 grew to sixty-five million dollars with an 8.3 percent increase over the previous year. With these changes and continued loyal customer support, positive earnings were re-established in 1998 following the losses of the corporate fire and the Waverly flood.

It was June 3, 1998 and Jack turned seventy years old. Babs recalled what he wanted most for his birthday was to go fishing at the cabin. Without ever losing his competitive spirit he expressed his plan to catch seventy fish that day. He told everyone, in the family, what he was going to do that day. He was recalled to have said, *"I am going to catch seventy fish today because it's my birthday! You watch and see."* Babs recalled they laughed and laughed. Since Jack had grown up with three sisters, he and his dad had enjoyed a few "boys only" opportunities. If Henry and Jack had a chance to escape and do a little something together, it was fishing. *"He really enjoyed doing that with his dad and later in life with the kids,"* Babs recalled. For Jack's birthday, the family left Point Pleasant and traveled to Jackson Lake. After getting settled in the cabin, with fishing pole and tackle box in hand he walked down to the lake. The family trailed along eager to see him enjoy his birthday. The weather was just right, not too hot or humid considering it was June. The fishing began. And the fish were really biting! The count began. By the end of the day, Jack had actually caught seventy fish. Babs recalled, with laughter, *"He did it! Jack fished and fished until he succeeded at this birthday goal of his. We all really, really enjoyed that day."*

Jack announced his retirement from City National Bank in 1998. Charles Lanham, the Executive Vice President of Ohio Valley Bank, at that time, had a few words to say about Jack's decision.

Dear Jack,

It is certainly with mixed emotions that I read the news article of your retirement from the City National Bank Board of Directors, and the Chairmanship of that official body. Jack, it has been an honor and a pleasure to work with you and compete against you during the last thirty years. You are one of the very few people I have known who could always see the fair and honorable way to address a situation. Your ability to achieve personal financial success and at the same time have a real sense of fairness toward your fellowman, your community and even your competitors has continually amazed me. You are the most financially successful individual I have known who was able to achieve that success without incurring the wrath and criticism of the public. You've dealt in politics, the business world, the church, the field of medicine, education and even banking without incurring any significant public criticism, a remarkable achievement. I am looking forward to a continuing working relationship.

Sincerely yours,
Charles C. Lanham

As Jack continued to be rewarded with blessings another window of giving reflected his bright journey and it involved the March of Dimes. What may first appear to a customer at Fruth Pharmacy as a ploy to get a dollar for a paper shoe, resulted in an astonishing financial contribution to this worthy organization. Through his encouraged support, Fruth Pharmacy associates, family members and friends raised a record twelve thousand dollars during the March of Dimes Tri-county Walk America event in 1999. Sporting Fruth Pharmacy custom designed Walk America t-shirts, the community walked to show support, three hundred strong. Jack continued efforts to fund this charitable organization through Fruth Pharmacy in preventing birth defects and infant mortality through the years.

As his blessed journey continued, a modest man enjoyed more fishing, less time at the office (although he still went in everyday) and more awards. In 1999, Jack was awarded the Ernst & Young Entrepreneur of the Year. This is the world's most prestigious business award for entrepreneurs. As the first and only truly global award of its kind, Entrepreneur Of The Year celebrates those who are building and leading successful, growing and dynamic businesses, recognizing them through regional, national and global awards programs in more than 140 cities and in more than 50 nations. Jack continued to be awarded many more honors of which were the West Virginia Entrepreneur of the Year Lifetime Achievement Award and the Distinguished West Virginia Award by Governor Cecil Underwood.

Although not all-inclusive, this brings the decade of the 1990s to a successful destination, despite a few hurdles. But, he's not finished yet. There are four more Fruth Pharmacys to open, the introduction of a stand-alone gift store, awards to be won, highways to be built, and more fish to be caught.

The Journey Leads To Higher Ground

"Jack Fruth was the most tender-hearted, caring person that I have ever had the privilege to have known. He truly cared about the health and welfare of people and their families," Ruth Kinnard, CPhT

This decade begins without the overshadowing knowledge that we would suffer such a tremendous loss midway. How could we have known? How could *he* have known? One thing we do know, and that was he lived his life in such a manner that he was *ready*. He was asked an interesting question during an interview with Patty Wade. She asked him, "How long have you been a Christian, Jack?" He smiled and seemed a bit shy with his response. Jack had this to say:

> I know a lot of people will say at such and such a time, on such and such a day, I became a Christian. Well, it wasn't like that for me. I look back over my life and I couldn't tell you the instant that I became a Christian. I'd like to think that I was always a Christian. Often times I think that when you are exposed to a Christian life growing up and are encouraged to go to church then you are influenced all along the way. I know

there's a time you are baptized. But I don't count that as the time. I felt like a Christian before I was baptized. Getting baptized was just something that occurred in a Christian's life. I don't see how you can totally separate a before and after.

This new decade had begun and business continued as usual. Jack was awarded the Marshall University Business Hall of Fame Award in 2000. Four new stores were on the docket to open, the next of which was the twenty-second Fruth Pharmacy[27] in Nelsonville, Ohio. This store, housed in a former Kroger building, offered a unique opportunity to give the folks in a rural area an option for not only prescription filling but also basic consumer goods and services. Again Jack placed stores in locations that were a bit off the beaten path. With ample parking and a drive-thru window, this store was another example of typical Fruth footprint. Though business would not serve to be as strong as many of the other Fruth stores, the Nelsonville Fruth was a successful endeavor.

With his giving nature and generous actions, Jack again shared in the form of educational assistance. Fruth Pharmacy announced a new scholarship that was awarded to Doug Wilson, a 2000 graduate of Point Pleasant High School. Doug became the first recipient of the scholarship for a full-time Mason County student to continue their education after high school by attending the Marshall Mid-Ohio Valley Center. Babs stated, "Jack and I sincerely hope that other Mason County citizens, businesses and industries join with us in encouraging young people to further their education." The Fruths also established an athletic scholarship for women at Marshall University and a scholarship for the Meigs County Center of the University of Rio Grande.

---

[27] *In consideration of the date on which this book was written, store #22 operates at 10 West Washington Street in Nelsonville, Ohio.*

In an effort to explore the potential for the first non-pharmacy operation, Fruth Pharmacy opened the Honey Bear Tree in early 2000. Once located at 909 Cross Lanes Drive in Cross Lanes, West Virginia. They offered gift items, discount greeting cards and floral arrangements. The building was a former Rite Aid drugstore. Rooms were sectioned off and various product lines including Yankee Candles and Precious Moments which were decoratively displayed on dark cabinetry with task lighting for emphasis on each product line. Although there was ample space for growth, considering the nine thousand-five hundred square foot gift floor, the customer base was never achieved. Despite much thought and investment, the Honey Bear Tree failed.

Fruth forged forward to better serve customers in 2000 by adding drive-thru windows at nine existing Fruth Pharmacy locations. The point of sale system continued to help customize the inventory to suit the consumers' needs. As a result of these measures, as well as the continued efforts in quality customer service, sales approached eighty million dollars in fiscal year 2000. With this increase in revenue, Jack and others considered what else could be done, in addition to existing advertising measures, to increase sales even more. This brought the introduction of television advertisements to Fruth Pharmacy. The decision was made to give it a try. They did. The first television commercial advertised a Christmas tree stand. This resulted in a large number of customers being pleased with the commercials and reportedly buying the products they had seen on television. The decision was made to eliminate one circular each quarter and put a television ad in its place. This redistribution of funds proved efficient. Fruth Pharmacy aired television commercials during morning talk shows and evening news programs just before major holidays. As a result, Christmas sales improved twenty percent; Valentine's Day sales improved eighteen percent resulting in overall sales for the fiscal 2001 increasing by 13.2 percent to ninety million dollars.

The television exposure led to Fruth Pharmacy offering an "Ask Your Pharmacist" segment as well. C.K. Babcock, PharmD served via this media and represented Fruth Pharmacy with helpful, knowledgeable prescription advice to phone-in viewers.

At the end of June 2002, Fruth Pharmacy revealed annual sales topping the one hundred million dollar mark for the first time, reaching one hundred and five million dollars. This was a 10.5 percent increase over the previous year. And Jack's blessed journey ventured forward. With three more stores to introduce, he continued. The twenty-third Fruth Pharmacy[28] opened in Scott Depot, West Virginia. This one was unique in origination because it was the first store that offered a 340B clinic through Family Care serviced by Fruth Pharmacy. The 340B clinic offered those with less than favorable financial resources an estimated savings of between twenty to fifty percent on the cost of prescription medications. With the escalating costs of prescription drugs, Fruth Pharmacy was proactive and searched for solutions, which better served all members of the community. The 340B clinic was a prime example of such efforts.

With 2002 came a remodel of the first Fruth Pharmacy in Point Pleasant, West Virginia. This remodel included a complete store makeover and the addition of a drive-thru window for prescription pick-up. Jack took great pride in the Point Pleasant store. Not that he didn't take great pride in all the store locations he did, but this one was particularly special. After all it was his first pharmacy, the one from which sprung all the others. Another proof that Jack was moving in the right direction came in 2002. The Drug Store News annual report of the chain drug store industry rated Fruth Pharmacy as the thirty-second largest retail drug chain the in the United States in dollars of retail sales and Fruth Pharmacy tied for thirty-first in number of retail locations.

---

[28] *In consideration of the date on which this book was written, store #22 operates at 4012 Teays Valley Road in Scott Depot, West Virginia.*

In November of 2002, Fruth Pharmacy celebrated 50 years of operation with an anniversary event. Jack was seventy-four years old and still worked every day. For the anniversary event, he visited each and every Fruth pharmacy. A table was dressed and set at the front of the store. Refreshments were served to customers and Jack was present to show his appreciation for their patronage, pose for photographs and shake hands. As evidenced in the beginning of the book, he was more than gracious to smile and sign or just stand and chat with customers and employees.

On the home front, he was more than gracious about manning the grill. He had developed a liking to cooking. Which was not necessarily a common task for Jack. Babs prepared all the meals for the family throughout the years. His role had been the provider. Though he loved to spend time fishing and enjoying the woods, he suffered from allergies so the great 'green' outdoors was not always his advocate. Which proved to serve him in that he never had the task of lawn mowing or hedge trimming as an adult. That didn't stop him from trying. He wanted to undertake some outside chores, Babs recalled, in the late 1950s. His father was very capable of maintaining all those rental properties. Henry mowed and had done all sorts of chores. But Jack was allergic to grass and if he took an antihistamine they made him hyper. After one day of yard work, all those years of childhood misery due to mowing were rekindled. After that, he left outside maintenance for others to complete. But he later did prevail when he became what Babs referred to as the grill chief. He loved it. He started doing a little cooking, first at home. He would experiment with scrambled eggs. They were his specialty. He would add a little of this and a little of that. He gained some confidence, which led to grill duty at the cabin. Babs recalled he said, "You know what? I just might take a few cooking lessons. I am enjoying this." She said they all laughed and let him continue his exploration of the culinary arts. He didn't get to those cooking lessons, but he pleased the family without ever having done so.

His journey needed a new highway on which to safely travel. Jack knew it. Every person who had ever driven on Route 35 from Point Pleasant to Charleston, West Virginia knew it. It took Jack's determination to get it started. Jack worked tirelessly with Charles Lanham and many others on the project—hours upon hours, years upon years. The day had come and in 2004 Governor Wise signed a proclamation that made the signage, Fruth-Lanham Highway, official in a ceremony at the Point Pleasant Moose Lodge. The Governor had this to say:

> They (Jack Fruth and Charles Lanham) represent the best to me of community spirit. They share a love of community and common values for the improvement of Mason County.

Over the years, millions of federal dollars had been committed to Route 35. It was Jack and Charles' combined hope that the availability of funds would have continued until a completed union between Putnam County and the Silver Memorial Bridge was in place—a completed four-lane highway. Their sincere intention was for a passageway that would not only be safe for local residents but also for those traveling through West Virginia. Charles Lanham, with regret, reflected on the incomplete project during an interview. Mr. Lanham said, *"I feel confident in saying that if Jack Fruth were living today, the Fruth-Lanham Highway would be completed."*

Governor Bob Wise signing the proclamation
for the Fruth-Lanham Highway

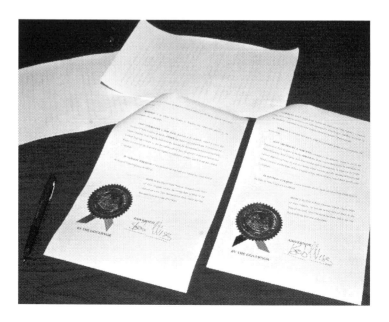

Babs and Jack Fruth, Bob Wise, 2004,
Fruth-Lanham Highway ceremony

In 2005, Jack Edward Fruth completed his blessed journey and did so with the grace and dignity that not many have ever done before him. On July 19, 2005 Jack left our earthly home to join his spiritual Grace. At his final ceremony[29], we shared a lesson, Proverbs 3:1-15, from the Old Testament. Pastor James H. Lewis read a poem "The Challenge" by Heartsill Wilson. After sharing the 23rd Psalm, led by Reverend Richard K. DeQuasie, he then read from the New Testament, Ephesians 2:1-10. As the service progressed, we shared the gospel lesson, Luke 24: 13-35 followed by the sermon for the service. John Fruth, Don Pullin, Reverend Steven Dorsey and Senator Charles Lanham

---

[29]   *Written as memories recalled by the author, Angie Johnson.*

gave witness as they spoke from their hearts with memories of Jack Fruth. I cannot recall one tearless eye in the chapel that day. Following their emotional deliveries of tender words, we joined to sing a congregational hymn, the Hymn of Promise from page 707 in the Trinity hymnal. The pews were full—overfilled as I recall. Folks were not only physically close due to the large number present but also emotionally contiguous—we were grieving in his absence. Reverend Richard K. DeQuasie led us through the Prayer of Thanksgiving followed by the Lord's Prayer. In the dismissal of the ceremony, a final blessing was delivered. This was it—the time had arrived for the pallbearers to take their place. Eight men, Laddie Burdette, Bob Messick, Joe Ellison, Bruce Scarberry, Paul Skinner, Jeff Smith, David Jenkins and Mike Lieving, respectfully carried the man we all had come to love more than I can find the words with which to explain. Jack Fruth was a good man—a great man even. We all hurt that day and as much as we did so for our personal loss, we did so more for his wife, children and grandchildren. In God's Promises, He gives grace for each trail, and courage for each sorrow, and faith to face in confidence a blessed, bright tomorrow. This day was one of those tomorrows. Each day we are continuing on and in doing so we are moving forward. As Jack was remembered to have said, *"The past is over, still, it is only the future that moves forward."*

The Trinity United Methodist Church surrounded all of us that day, with warm floors and comforting walls. Jack loved his church and church family. It could be said that 615 Viand Street in Point Pleasant had become his second home over the years and one that welcomed his final visit and his endearing guests. He was buried at the Kirkland Memorial Gardens in Point Pleasant, West Virginia with Masonic graveside and Minturn Lodge #19, A.F. & A.M. rites. There were thirteen honorary pallbearers of importance to mention. Those men were: Don Pullin, Charles Lanham, Oshel Craigo, Jim Divine, Jimmy Lewis, Dr. Barry

Dorsey, Bill Knight, Jack Buxton, Bob Wingett, Dallas Kayser, Mario Libertore, Dr. Aaron Boonsue and Dr. Young Choi.

While folks made an attempt to return to business as usual, it would never be usual again at Fruth Pharmacy. For Jack, everyone chipped in to do whatever was necessary to continue in his absence. The personnel at the corporate office were the hardest hit. They saw him, heard his voice and turned to him on a daily basis. The news spread quickly regarding his death; however, it took some time for everyone to know. While at a conference in Baltimore, a gentleman came running across the crowded room toward C.K. Babcock. He was talking before he reached him and this is how their conversation went:

> "Hey! Do you work for Fruth Pharmacy?" he boisterously asked as he kept his eyes on C.K.'s name badge. He was winded. When he got close enough he looked up and saw C.K.'s face (big smile and all). With eyes wide and a face full of curiosity he immediately asked, "How is Mr. Fruth?" With a tender turn C.K. told him that he was sad to say that he had passed away one year ago. The gentleman was devastated. He told C.K. that Mr. Fruth was one of the greatest men that he had ever known. He expressed his condolences and then proceeded to share a story. He said, "I sat on a board of directors with Mr. Fruth. I was by far one of the least financially privileged among the group. Several of the people ran businesses that easily exceeded one hundred million dollars per year. Toward the end of the meeting, an argument broke out about how we should finish the project. We could meet the project's standard within the ten thousand dollar budget or we could go slightly over budget and extend the time frame but the

outcome would better serve the project. The discussion got heated, to put it mildly, and tempers were lost. There was yelling and screaming. When we, on both sides of the argument, slowed down long enough to allow a breather, one of the men interjected. He turned to Jack and said, 'What do you think, Jack?' I hadn't even noticed that Jack was sitting there all this time just as quiet as a church mouse. He was calm, cool and collected. I suppose he had just been taking it all in, evaluating the near hostile situation, considering an escape route. I don't know. He was just interesting in his mannerisms. He had a thick-tongued accent, the West Virginia sort. He said, 'Well if it were my momma, I would want it done this way.' Everyone at the table immediately relaxed. The tension left that room quicker than you could blink your eye. There was no need to further discuss the matter. With those few words, from a very wise man, we reached an agreement. Jack was like a farmer who worked his entire life and then shared his knowledge methodically. One sentence from that man meant more than the thirty minutes of ranting from a room full of strong-minded, wealthy men."

In Mr. Fruth's absence, C.K. as well as other loyal employees continued to attend pharmaceutical conferences on behalf of Fruth Pharmacy. With continued enquiries coming in from concerned folks regarding his absence, these first months were the most difficult to endure. Their mentor was gone. Meeting this gentleman as he came running across a crowded room to talk about Mr. Fruth with such admiration was just another example of how his blessed journey will continue forever.

In continuing forward, the twenty-fourth Fruth Pharmacy[30] opened in Cross Lanes, West Virginia. This was the first store to open with a double drive-thru window to service the pharmacy department. A short time after that the twenty-fifth and final Fruth Pharmacy[31] opened in Charleston, West Virginia. This was a completely unique footprint for the company, a much smaller format. With twenty five hundred square feet, a downtown city street location and reduced hours of operation, this would be the first Fruth Express to join the chain—a caboose so to speak. This store became a reality because of a pharmacist named Sam Arco. Sam had worked for Donnie Neurman, R.Ph., who owned two Medicine Shoppe pharmacies in Charleston, one across the street from what became the Fruth Express and one in Kanawha City. Rite Aid bought both of Donnie's stores. In doing so, Rite Aid made the decision to close the downtown store, Sam's store, leaving many lifelong patrons without local prescription services. Sam didn't want to transfer to another area. He had worked downtown for years and had an intimate relationship with his patients. Sam did his homework and called Laddie Burdette to see if there was anything he could do. Could Fruth Pharmacy work something out to save his patients and his store? He was willing to try. He knew that both Mr. Fruth and Laddie had trusted reputations and sincere caring hearts for people and the pharmacy community. He knew that Laddie, in Mr. Fruth's absence, continued to loyally serve Fruth Pharmacy. Sam called him. In doing his homework, Sam learned that it just so happened a vacant building was awaiting a new tenant just across the street from the Medicine Shoppe. He thought it would be the perfect location for Fruth Pharmacy to set up shop. Laddie agreed to lease the vacant building and within

---

[30] *In consideration of the date on which this book was written, store #24 operates at 5455F Big Tyler Road in Cross Lanes, West Virginia.*

[31] *In consideration of the date on which this book was written, store #25 operates at 701 Lee Street East in Charleston, West Virginia.*

three months the store opened. Fruth Pharmacy even employed Sam at store #14 during that transition time so that he didn't lose any hours of employment. Today this store operates under the caring hand of Sam Arco and staff. As a result, the downtown community, in Charleston, West Virginia, is better served thanks to the willingness of Laddie to listen and the reputation that Mr. Fruth had established along his journey for his company, Fruth Pharmacy.

The face of pharmacy changed much during this decade with decreased reimbursements and more and more required red tape in dealing with the growing Medicaid and Medicare population. These changes have dramatically affected the national landscape of pharmacy. The management team at Fruth stayed innovative with new ways to attract customers via disease state management, West Virginia State employees Face To Face Program and immunization services. Keeping with Mr. Fruth's influence in government activities, after he stepped down from the West Virginia Board of Pharmacy, Laddie Burdette was appointed his position. Mr. Fruth believed that you should be physically active in leadership roles to better your odds of influencing a workable outcome for those who become recipients of such important decisions. He guarded the profession of pharmacy, from every angle, with every available resource. He encouraged Laddie, Eric and C.K. to become and remain active members of governing bodies to support and protect pharmacists. He was a pharmacist at heart and continued to shelter fellow colleagues from all possible vantage points. He encouraged his pharmacists, at store level, to participate in NACDS (National Association of Chain Drug Stores), NCPA (National Community Pharmacist's Association) and many other professional organizations.

In 2008, the Fruth family majority owners in the business made the decision to become more actively involved in the company. Three members were elected to the board of directors and included:

John Fruth, James Rossi (nephew) and Lynne Fruth. These three new members joined existing members: Babs Fruth, Mike Fruth, Laddie Burdette and Bob Messick. With a final growth of Fruth Pharmacy totaling six hundred plus employees, twenty-five pharmacies (sixteen in West Virginia and nine in Ohio), a corporate office and two warehouses, this group had their hands full.

Today the challenges are even greater, with multiple personnel exchanges and new hurdles in pharmaceutical care. But, with Lynne Fruth as acting President and Chairman of the Board of Fruth Pharmacy, Inc., she continues with one primary goal, that being the continued success of a company that her father built. Her father's dream has become her focus. With her mother, Babs, at her side accompanied by the support of the entire Fruth family, the business is moving forward. Apart, with much distance from the past, Fruth Pharmacy moves into a financially successful future—after all a great man once said, "along this journey in our lives, the future is all that moves forward."

PART II

A Journey of Giving Continues Through Photographs and Memories

Henrietta and Jack Fruth, 1929, Mason, West Virginia

Jack and Henrietta Fruth during the mid 1930s

Frances "Babs" Rhodes, Senior High School

Fruth at Greenbrier Military School

Jack E. Fruth at Greenbrier Military School.

Jack Edward Fruth, Senior High School

Frances "Babs" Rhodes, Ohio State University Graduation

Babs and Jack, 1950-51 Ohio State University Fraternity Dance

Marjorie Fruth, Fruth Pharmacy #1 in Point Pleasant, West Virginia

2501-1/2 Lincoln Avenue. Jack and Babs' first house in
Point Pleasant, West Virginia

Kathyrn Fruth, Henrietta Rossi, Emogene Crooks, Marjorie Fruth
and Jack Fruth mid 1960s

Jack Fruth revisited the Greenbrier Military School campus, 1964

Babs, Carol, Joan, Mike, Lynne and John Fruth. 1965

The Fruth Family

The Fruth family in 1968

Jack E. Fruth, 1975

Babs and Jack Fruth, 1976

Babs, Jack, Stephanie and Nicole, 1980s

Kathyrn, Jack and Henrietta, 1995

Babs and Jack Fruth at the John Marshall Society Dinner, 04-30-98

Jack Fruth with his beloved sisters

Babs, Jack and Joan Fruth, 1991

Jack and his grandson, Michael, mid 1990s

Oshel Craigo, Jack and Governor Bob Wise, 12-30-00

Babs and Jack Fruth celebrating the 50th Anniversary of Fruth Pharmacy, 2002

Jack and Babs Fruth

Jack Fruth, Henrietta Fruth Rossi and Louis Rossi, 12-30-00

The Fruth Family, 2005

Angie Johnson, R.Ph.

As a supreme example of Jack Fruth's compassion for his fellowman, I want to share this extremely sensitive story with you. David Jenkins was gracious enough to open his heart and relive his family tragedy, and for that I am most humbly appreciative. He recollected this very sad experience in order to give Mr. Fruth glory, a man he grew to respect, honor and love.

COSTA RICA

"My name is David Jenkins and this is my family's story," David Jenkins.

I worked for Revco in the early 1980s. The pharmacist there was Steve Wilson. He and I worked together for a time. He ran the pharmacy department and I worked the front-end of the store. He left Revco in Chesapeake, Ohio to work for Geary Spencer, R.Ph., in Huntington, West Virginia. Geary and Mr. Fruth were business partners. Steve told Geary about me and I was then hired by Fruth in 1982. Throughout my years with Fruth, I managed six different stores and started buying merchandise along the way. Mr. Fruth transferred me to the corporate office in 1996 as a buyer for the company and today I am still there. I had no idea the impact that taking a job with Fruth Pharmacy would have on my family until my father made a visit to Costa Rica.

After forty-one years of employment, my father retired from Kroger in 2001. He was very active with his church family prior to retiring; however, it was after retiring that he became much more involved with his extended church family. He began doing a lot of missionary work and traveling with the First United Methodist Church in Ashland, Kentucky. He made three trips to Costa Rica. It was his third trip, in January 2001 that changed our lives forever. He was with the church group and they had been enjoying fellowship with the local folks of Costa Rica one evening when he fell. He gathered himself, said he was fine, brushed off the incident, and walked back to his room. When he arrived there, he said that he did have a slight headache so he took a couple Tylenol for it and went to sleep.

The next morning they could not wake him. We got a phone call. As it turned out, the fall had resulted in a subdural hematoma. A subdural hematoma is a collection of blood on the surface of the brain. These injuries are among the deadliest of all head injuries. The fall causes the injury; the bleeding then fills the brain area rapidly, compressing brain tissue. The symptoms include: confused speech, difficulty with balance or walking, headache, and loss of consciousness just to mention a few. A subdural hematoma is an emergency condition in which surgery is needed to reduce the pressure within the brain. The surgery may involve drilling a small hole in the skull to allow blood to drain, thereby relieving the pressure on the brain. If the clot has solidified, a craniotomy is required, which creates a larger opening in the skull through which the clot is removed. The outlook following a subdural hematoma varies widely depending on type and location of the injury, the size of the blood collection, how quickly treatment is obtained, and quality of health care at hand.

Here my dad was, in a third-world country just about three hours from the nearest city in Costa Rica that was San Jose, with a potentially fatal head injury and in need of brain surgery. The medics were called. They transported him to Clinica Biblica hospital in San Jose and did emergency brain surgery in an attempt to save his life. My mother (Sue Jenkins), my two sisters (Debbie Payne and Rae Ann Mains) and I made arrangements to fly to Costa Rica the day after we received the news. We then spent the next sixteen days in Costa Rica, at our father's bedside. He was in a coma and his condition was very touch and go for a while. Our family faced a difficult situation with our father's life in jeopardy. We prayed.

The consideration of insurance coverage was not even a factor. After all, my dad had worked at Kroger for forty-one years with a flawless record of employment. He was eligible for and did have Medicare coverage with supplemental Kroger insurance to pick up the balance. It was not until the hospital administration approached us to inquire how we intended to pay the bill that we learned those insurances were not billable by a medical facility outside the United States. In shock, I find myself in a situation where I am talking with the administrative staff at Clinica Biblica in San Jose, Costa Rica trying desperately to find a way to pay the existing hospital bill, as well as future treatments and charges. At this point, not only is my father in a physically vulnerable position, he is also financially vulnerable. To further intensify our predicament we learn that they are not going to let any of us leave the country without first paying this bill. I regrouped with my mother and two sisters. We each paid Clinica Biblica what we could to the limits of our credit cards. And still, that was not enough to allow us to leave.

I had kept in touch with folks at work via Bob Messick who was, at that time, the CFO of Fruth Pharmacy and with my family through email messages. Mr. Fruth had checked-in with Bob to see how things were going during those days that I was away from my job at the corporate office. I started at Fruth in 1982. Mr. Fruth and I had worked together for many years. It wasn't until this time that I realized his level of greatness. Bob had sat down with Mr. Fruth and explained my family's crisis. Mr. Fruth granted permission for me to use the Fruth company credit card to settle the remainder of the bill at Clinica Biblica. This gave us tremendous peace of mind knowing we could now bring our father home. Meanwhile back at home, other family members (Tim Mains and Mike Payne) were not only busy taking care of their own families but also were finding a hospital close to home for Dad, making arrangements for a medical jet equipped with a pilot, co-pilot, physician, two males nurses, me, Mom and Dad so that we could get home. This was sixteen days later and my dad was still in a coma. We flew non-stop from Costa Rica to Huntington, West Virginia.

Once we returned home, the church family got busy. They had all sorts of fund raising events from pancake breakfasts and dinners to musical concerts in an effort to repay Mr. Fruth. The bill was well over one hundred thousand dollars. This was a trying time for all of us. Through the help of the church and the community, we were able to pay back the money in full that Mr. Fruth had gifted. Our family will never forget his graceful generosity that changed our lives forever. When I came back to work after sixteen days of absence and went to our human resource department at Fruth to turn in my vacation time Mr. Fruth interceded to say, "No. It is not necessary." He told me that I still had my two weeks vacation and not to worry about anything else for a while. He was a great man, a man of generosity and compassion.

The Fruth employees also collected money to help with my family's phone charges, which were well over six hundred dollars. I specifically remember the day that I was standing on the steps at Fruth and Eric Lambert, at that time Director of Pharmacy at Fruth, was passing by on his way home and said he had heard what happened and he gifted my family a contribution. It's funny too, as if Mr. Fruth had not gone above and beyond to save my family, he too gave a donation. He personally donated one thousand dollars.

My father has since passed but was able to live several years with a good fight. His mind was never the same after the fall in Costa Rica. His motor function was damaged as well; he could walk but only with assistance. My mother was able to keep him at home for a year and a half and then he was placed in a nursing home. He resided there for the remaining seven years of his life. But before the nursing home, he and my mother came to the Fruth corporate office. They wanted to thank Mr. Fruth in person. They did. I was asked what one word or sentence best described Mr. Fruth. My answer is, without hesitation: Integrity. He sure meant a lot to me.

THE FRUTH CHILDREN

In an interview with Patty Wade on the God is Good local television program, Jack said, *"People will often ask about my business success and about various accomplishments but I am most proud of my children above anything else. With five children and eight grandchildren, God has blessed us many times."*

After much consideration about how and where to share more about the children, it seemed only natural to let them speak for themselves. Throughout the next several pages, they share candid memories of their years growing up under the guardianship of two loving parents, Jack and Babs Fruth. From the oldest son, Mike, to the youngest son, John, they encompass the years of their childhood. My wish would be for you to hear their stories in their own voices. Each of Jack and Babs' children were unique as they reflected on their childhood. I watched and listened as they remembered younger days through smile-filled faces and at times tear-filled eyes. I recall each one of them to be so very proud of both parents and appreciative to have had such a blessed childhood. We begin with Mike.

MIKE'S VOICE

My dad always said, *"Pick a career that you enjoy doing everyday, son, and not because of any associated financial reward. That way you will be successful in what you do,"* Michael Edward Fruth.

When I was growing up, I would spend a lot of time at the store with my dad. Over the years it only made sense for me to become a pharmacist—like my dad. He never pressured me to do so. His advice was to find a career that I enjoyed and do it. Do it because it is a career that you enjoy and not because of any associated financial reward. He would say to me, 'Don't be in a job your entire life that you hate.' He always believed that if you liked what you did then you would be successful.

I enjoyed spending time at the store. Dad was there, of course, but also my grandmother, aunt(s), and many a time my brothers and sisters. It was a second home. I had, well we all had, a lot of support while growing up. We had a great family life—immediate and extended. The grandchildren had that same support system, all eight of them. Dad very much loved and unconditionally supported all of us.

I graduated from Ohio Northern Raabe College of Pharmacy in Ada, Ohio with a Bachelor of Science Degree in Pharmacy. I have returned to campus on several occasions. I enjoy taking part in ONU's Mentor Program and believe it is very important. One should always give back to the community and not just financially but of your time. Dad always did. For the mentor dinner, about seventy to one hundred students attend. Each mentor is assigned anywhere from one to three students. We share dinner with the students, offer advice and our time for any questions they may have or for direction they may need. It is very rewarding. It's a giving session. I try to attend ONU's career day too. Fruth Pharmacy is represented there with a booth, company information and potential employment opportunities for prospective graduating pharmacy students. I have participated in the ONU golf outing a few times—participation matters. Dad always thought so.

One of the most important things that my dad taught me about pharmacy was that it is a giving profession. As a kid, I cannot count the times my dad was called after hours or on a holiday to open the store and dispense medication to a sick child or adult. Many of those times, I went with him. And, you know what? He never minded to do it. He was always pleased to have been a part of helping someone else feel better. When you look at all the things that my Dad was involved in, he always tried to help the individual, the community and or the state. He never had a personal agenda—public service was always number one.

There were a few employees, at the store in Point Pleasant, whom I recall as fixtures. The first person that comes to my mind is Ruth Flowers and she still works there. She was always great and over the years has become more special and just such a resonating part of that store. Another lady that I recall was Mabel Yeager. She was always at the front counter to say hello and goodbye and I came and went a bunch. She was a cashier for Dad and was a special person and an important part of the store. And then there was Jack Scarberry. He was a stock guy/merchandiser and really just a jack-of-all-trades. I enjoyed talking with him over the years. He did a great job working at the store.

As kids growing up in Point Pleasant, we were just into about everything. I am sure the cumulative number of stitches that we all endured would total in the hundreds. We did a lot of ice-skating and sleigh riding in the winter at Roseberry's Farm. It was just down and over the hill from our neighborhood. In the summer, we built all sorts of things from miniature golf courses (and I am sure my sisters will talk about that) to concession stands (mostly soda fountain type treats) in our yard at the house. We fished a lot too. Dad loved fishing with the family. That was one of his favorite pastimes. Playing cards was another popular thing that the family enjoyed doing together. And we still do. We play a few card games: hearts (my favorite) and yuker or thirty-one (their favorite). There were a lot of sports activities too. I played baseball until I was about twelve years old. I still coach softball and enjoy golf. Our Fruth Pharmacy women's softball team is an upper tier team. We play mainly in Columbus and Cincinnati. I still enjoy officiating football and softball games at the high school level. That's a great way to give back to the local community and a small way to volunteer my time for a good cause. In all forms from athletics to scholastics, kids need a lot of support from adults. Time is an important contribution. I try to be thoughtful toward the kids. My dad always was and he knew it mattered.

I live in Wellston, Ohio and have for years. Another form of volunteer participation is with the Wellston Rotary. I have been active with this group for upwards of twenty years. Once a year, we embark on a fund raising event for the Rotary. It's called the Wellston Rotary Minstrel Show. My sister, Joan, participates as well. Mother has taken part in the last eight shows. She enjoys it. The show involves a skit, singing, an old-time screen set and any other props we can drum up. It's the Rotary's biggest single activity for the year. Practice begins around the first of February and takes place about three times per week. Any willing participant that is eighteen years or older is welcome to join in the event. The show runs from mid-March to April on a Thursday, Friday and Saturday. It's just another way to give back to the community. The Rotary, in turn, uses the revenue that the show generates to better the community. Our family enjoys and looks forward to it each year.

Family is just what *is* so important. It's the most valuable. My dad taught us that. We did a lot of things together while growing up. We do as much as we can together now as adults. I still work at the Fruth corporate office as the import and seasonal buyer. I also practice as a pharmacist at the store in Point Pleasant on a part-time basis. It is still very much a family business.

[Michael Edward Fruth, R.Ph. graduated from Ohio Northern University Raabe College of Pharmacy in Ada, Ohio with a Bachelor of Science in Pharmacy. Mike holds licensure to practice pharmacy in West Virginia and Ohio. He currently works as a practicing pharmacist on a part-time basis with Fruth Pharmacy. As well, he works at the corporate office on a daily basis and is the Vice President of Imports.]

JOAN'S VOICE

My dad always said to me:
*"Nobody ever said that you had to decide, when
you are eighteen years old, what you are going to
do for the rest of your life, Joan. Fifty percent of it
is showing up where you are supposed to be when
you are supposed to be there and doing what you are
supposed to do,"* Joan Elizabeth Fruth.

I recall the time my dad had bought an old drug store in Ironton, Ohio. I wasn't very old. Dad came home from work and asked if I wanted to go with him and Grandpa to take a look at the place. He would take me along on small trips from time to time. So I went. This happened each time he bought a new store. We would go over and he would walk every aisle while taking down all sorts of notes about future plans for it. He always kept a notebook. This particular pharmacy still had merchandise in it. My grandpa was the big merchandiser. He would want items stacked from floor to ceiling. We had driven the station wagon. So they decided it best to load the car with as much merchandise as we could, bring it back to the store in Point, and sell it off. My grandpa was like me. If he could fit one more tube of toothpaste, in a small space, then he would. We had that car packed and tight. This would have been fine except we had a flat tire on the way home. I was small and very tired because it was getting late. I just really didn't want to help. I had to. We pulled off the road. It was dark. Here we were halfway between Ironton and Point Pleasant. We had to unload all that merchandise, along the side of the road, to get to the spare tire that was inside the station wagon, under all the stuff. Then Dad had to change the tire or Grandpa; I can't recall which one of the two or both that did it. But *then* all the merchandise had to be reloaded back into the car before we could head for home. I'll never forget that trip.

There was another time when I went along. My Uncle Carl was a barber and had a shop on Main Street, in Point Pleasant. He called Dad one evening to ask if Dad would take a look at a building downtown that he was interested in buying. Carl did not drive. Dad hung up the phone, looked around for a taker to accompany him and he and I left to pick up Uncle Carl and go downtown. Uncle Carl owned a lot of rental properties. Carl had helped start a bank in Point Pleasant but that didn't mean he kept his money there. He had lived through the crash of 1929 and he really just did not trust banks with his money. He decided to buy this building downtown. It was near Vi's Beauty Shop. There were stairs that led up the side of the building to the top story. This is how you entered the apartment. It was part of the purchase, too. A lady lived there for years—maybe all her years. I just remember that she was always there. She paid thirty-five dollars per month. After Dad and Uncle Carl looked the place over and talked about the potential purchase, the decision was made. Uncle Carl bought the place. We got back in the car and Dad drove us back to Uncle Carl's house. We all went inside. Uncle Carl told me to sit down and wait because I wasn't leaving yet. He disappeared upstairs. I don't know where he had the money stuffed—not sure which room or if it may have been the attic. He came back downstairs and said that he had a chore for me. I was about fourteen or fifteen years old. Uncle Carl passed to me handfuls of cash—crumpled and unordered. He wanted it flattened and counted until it totaled fifteen thousand dollars—that was the cost to purchase the building. He said, 'Count to fifteen thousand and then stop.' I started with separating the ones, fives, tens and twenties into crumpled stacks. Then I smoothed, flattened and counted the money. He would check on me from time to time and say, "How much more do you need?" I just remember flattening and counting all that money and him keeping all of it at his house. That was an adventure.

My Grandpa was always doing business of some sort—buying property and selling things. He would always say to me, 'Now Joan, you don't horse trade.' He might go that day and make an offer. If they said, 'no,' then you would leave. That did not mean he wouldn't return the next day and make a different offer—but then again he may not.

I remember a time when I was about twelve years old and there was an emergency at the store. Margie Dennis was washing glasses at the soda fountain and she, broke one, cut her hand. In doing so, she had to leave and get stitches. Dad didn't have anyone else to work the soda counter. I mean he needed me to be alone, by myself, and work the entire soda fountain counter. I was very reluctant. But my dad was very convincing. He said, 'Now Joan, you know boys always come over and talk to the girls that work at the soda fountain.' And he thought that at age twelve that was going to be my driving incentive to go and do it. It even required that you wear a dress. I did it for my dad. So, that was my first day of work there and I stayed until 9:30 at night—alone the entire shift.

My twelfth year was filled with adventures. I had begged for a horse for as long as I could remember. My Mother said, 'When you turn twelve, you can get one.' I had done all sorts of chores—mowed grass, took out the trash, just anything to earn money. I had saved and saved. Well, my twelfth birthday arrived. I was ready to go buy the horse. My mother said to me,

'Well, Joan, we thought that you would be bigger by the time you turned twelve.' I threw the biggest fit there ever was! I had wanted a horse from the time that I could say horse, like since I was two years old. My parents finally gave in to my pleas and said that I could get one. I used the money that I had saved to buy grain, hay and supplies. The rent was nine-dollars per month at the Harmon Park Stables. We would do all sorts of chores there to get free rent too. We would wash the barn every summer. We moved sawdust around in the wheelbarrow from the stockpile to the barn stalls, whatever it took. We (Brenda Adkins, Angie Campbell and I) rode three hundred and sixty-five days a year, everyday rain or shine. We would ride from the horse stable to the store, tie the horses up behind the store and go inside for a drink at the soda fountain. Having a horse, when you were twelve, was like having your own car. We would ride those horses all over Point Pleasant. My horse was named Cochise. He was a paint horse, brown and white with a black mane and tail. One year Angie won a pony at Harmon Park. We would have horse shows and concessions there in the summer. We kept it in her backyard and rode that pony a long time after we outgrew it. We had a lot of fun with horses and ponies, great times.

Later in years much of our family entertainment came from times spent at the cabin at Jackson Lake. That's where I live now. On my dad's seventieth birthday, he wanted to go fishing. So, we did. The fish were really biting that day and thank heavens. He was so happy that day. Mom would go along, rarely dangle her pole in the water and mostly read a book while we fished. Dad would say to her, 'Now, Mother, you know that you just can't catch a fish if you don't put your line in the water!' She knew that. That day, she humored him and did fish because it was his birthday. I think she caught more fish that day than she ever had, about twenty. Dad caught his age in fish, seventy! That was a great day.

I remember the day that my dad and mom came to Mike and me and said, 'You two need to buy a house.' We were living in the apartment behind the Fruth Pharmacy in Wellston and had been for years. Mike was reluctant. He was quiet for a long time then he said, 'Okay. I will pay for it and sign but I am not looking!' So Mom, Dad and I set out to find a house in Wellston. Dad had a list with all the criteria written out and it included the things he felt a must for the new house. We found one on a corner, double lot in Wellston for sale by owner and just about five blocks from the store. The house was built in 1890 so it needed renovated. It was the one. My seventy-six year old carpenter, Thornton Wilson, got busy and eighteen months later it was ready. Mike and I had been on vacation in Myrtle Beach. I told him, 'When we get back, it is time to move into the house.' Mike said, 'Okay.' He still had not looked at it. We got all moved in and Mike still lives there. I share a home at Jackson Lake with Greg.

We garden, even now. Greg helps me. When I was young, my mom would let me pick out my own flowers. I loved pansies with the purple faces or the dark purple ones. We would come home and I would plant my own little garden. My grandfathers were both big gardeners. Dad was not. I had my first real vegetable garden when I was seven years old. I grew carrots and radishes. I still have the seed of a gardener. At the house in Wellston, I prepared the yard and put in a lot of plantings. Funny, Mike does the gardening there now. He didn't, at first, when I was there. At our home at Jackson Lake, Greg and I once planted one thousand bulbs! I love to be surrounded by flowers, plants, and animals. My dad would always say to me, 'Joan, do what you love because you spend so much time at it that you had better love it. If your heart is not in it, you'll never be good at it.' I would ask my dad, 'How do you know what you like if you like so many things?' He would say, 'Start with what you don't like—write those things down. That is seventy-five percent of the decision. Start there.'

He would say, 'You can do other things that you don't truly have a love for but you will only ever be mediocre at them if it's not your passion.'

The store was my dad's passion. He worked at what he loved which was offering services to people. I remember the first day that the store took in more money in one day (it was a Christmas Eve) than my dad had taken in the entire first year the store was open. That was a memorable day! Dad was so excited. It was the first ten thousand dollar day. He wrote that figure down in his notebook. He was excited, of course, that the business was doing so well but also at the sportsmanship of what that number implied. He would always say, 'The dollars and cents are just a way to keep score—to tell you if you are winning or losing the game.' My Dad didn't just want good for himself and his family. He wanted good for all. My grandmother Fruth was like that. She would always say, 'You need a job because it is your contribution to society. Whether you need the money or not, you should always be a giving, responsible person.' My dad must have heard that a lot himself growing up. He continued to work many years after he could have retired. He enjoyed being a giving person.

In times when I struggled through one situation or another, I always looked to my dad for advice. He was great at giving advice. He told me, 'Never quit, Joan. Always persevere and it will all be okay in the end. Just never give up, never.'

[Joan Elizabeth Fruth graduated from Marshall University with a Bachelor's Degree in 1983 and a Masters in Sports Medicine in 1986. She currently works for Fruth Pharmacy as a Project Specialist. In the past, Joan competed in various National and World Power Lifting Championships. She was the first female lifting competitor in the State of West Virginia. This led to worldwide lifting competitions that took her to Los Angeles, California. In May of 1980, Joan became the first Women's World Power Lifting Champion, ever. Throughout her career, Joan set twenty-seven world records. She went forward to then compete in bodybuilding. Joan later judged bodybuilding and coached all forms of strength training. Today she is a Certified Strength and Conditioning Specialist (CSCS) through the National Strength and Conditioning Association (NSCA).]

CAROL'S VOICE

"The two people that I most admire and respect, in all my life, are my parents—my mother and my dad," Carol Rhodes Fruth.

It was the simplest things that made my dad laugh. He was a happy man. He had much more time for the simple things later in his life. He worked less then. We were fishing one time on Jackson Lake, where the cabins are. Joan and I were out in this johnboat with Dad when the rain casually began to fall. Dad threw in a line and caught one. A little time passed and I did the same. Joan wasn't happy—she didn't catch one. Even then, we were still playfully competitive. Dad and I were all smiles with the light rain, it wasn't bothering us at all. But then it began to pour buckets of rain. We couldn't even get back to the shore it was raining so much. Dad began to laugh. He laughed so hard that his body shook like Santa Claus. I think about it now and I laugh when remembering him like that. I see a man with so much wealth and success fishing from a small johnboat, in the rain with his daughters. He was happy that day.

Even when Dad would take the grandchildren fishing, he would set the mood for a little competitive sporting. He would tease that they had not caught as many fish as he had. He would ask them all sorts of questions, 'Did you spit on the mealworm before you put it on the hook? Are you using a bobber? Count my fish. I have caught more than you!' All the while, he would laugh as they began to think about strategies by which to catch more fish than him. After all, that was the purpose of the tease—he was teaching them.

He participated in some simple things throughout my childhood and those in which he did, I clearly remember. One year he asked Mother for a toboggan for Christmas. Well, of course, Mother was going to make sure he got one. She took us shopping and purchased what was thought to be the perfect one. It was a large one—big enough to hold all of us! That sled had three curved runners and a strong rope long enough for him to pull us back up the snow covered hills. When the snow came, we were ready. Dad would give us a big push to start and then he would jump on too! That was fun. Mother didn't know he actually wanted a hat for Christmas. He teased her for years over that toboggan. He loved to joke with her. My parents had good years, great years and then even better years together. He adored her. When he arrived home from work everyone got hugs and kisses. We thought everyone lived like that.

Dad had a habit of splitting his pants. It just happened to him. He would come home from work and tell Mother what he had done. She would say, 'Jack!' And he would just laugh. She would neatly mend them for him—time and time again. She was a great seamstress. Dad always dressed in a shirt and tie for work. He would come into our rooms sometimes to say goodbye in the mornings. One morning I said, 'Dad you have a spot on your shirt.' He said, 'I know but your mother is sleeping and I don't want to wake her by changing it.' That was my dad.

He always had the crummy car. Mother drove the nice one. The kids on the street would push it for him when it wouldn't take off. That happened more than once. Even after the reverse was gone out of it, he still drove it until a hole revealed the pavement through the floorboard. The rust won the battle.

There were five of us children, so we would get creative sometimes and come up with get rich schemes. To this day, I have no idea what we were going to get rich for or what we would have bought if we had done so, but nonetheless it was fun. In doing so, I suppose it gave us a task to complete, a project so to speak. One that I particularly remember was our petting zoo. We planned it all out. We built cages for animals out of all sorts of materials. We thought and thought about where to get the animals. I can't remember whose idea it was to check out the newspaper for free pets, but that is what we did. We answered the Point Pleasant Register's giveaway ads for pets, all kinds. We called, located where they lived, and walked to pick them up. We had a bunch of animals. Our uncle had an empty house in Mossman Circle. We decided to store the animals there until we were completely ready to open up our petting zoo. When uncle Louis found out, we were in some serious trouble and he had a house full of animals!

We built a miniature golf course in the backyard one summer. We were going to charge the neighborhood kids to play. We really worked on it. That was when John got hit in the head with a hatchet during construction. John was scooping out a tunnel and Lynne was digging a sand trap. In doing so, she swung down and chopped John. We had to call grandmother Fruth. She threw a fit! John returned from the hospital with stitches that day.

We were playing in the backyard one day when Lynne pushed her hand through a glass pane. Our neighbor, Mrs. Casto, came to her rescue. Lynne was impressed when she used one of her nice washcloths to stop the bleeding. It seems we were always getting into things. It wasn't any different when we visited Dad at the pharmacy either. Lynne cut his phone cord once, the curly part. I can't remember if that was before or after she was vacuuming and let the bag burst. Dust and dirt went all over the pharmacy. And, there was the time when John was swinging a one-gallon jug of sticky cough syrup around and around when the lid came off. It spilled all down his winter coat and onto the floor. But you know what? Dad never made us leave. Not once. We might have gotten moved to another chore, but we never got kicked out.

As soon as you could count change back to a customer, you could stand at the counter and help Dad's clerk. That was a big reward to us. Dad let us maintain the gumball machines in the pharmacy. We were allowed to pick out the candy, service the refills and keep the money. We counted a lot of change. We would put it in paper rolls and then take it to the bank.

We took a vacation in the summer and always to a state park. Those were good times. Dad loved the water. He taught all of us how to swim and the grandchildren too. He loved to tell jokes in the car. He had a couple of regular ones that we all heard more than once. One was the falling rock story. It would take several hours to reach our vacation destination, so there was time. As we got farther into the hills of West Virginia, we would begin to see signs that read: Watch Out For Falling Rock. Dad would go into great detail and length about this Indian warrior brave, named Falling Rock, who had traveled and then traveled farther. That brave had conquered territories and acquired treasures of great value. He was to be watched out for because he was a great Indian warrior and feared by all who crossed his path. He had even scalped people. He told us that was why when you travel through West Virginia you see signs that read: Watch Out For Falling Rock. He had us convinced, at least for a little while anyway.

And the second one that I most recall is: Two Men In The Submarine. He would get us all primed and ready to pay close attention to him. So we did. He would explain the depths of the ocean, the time of year, the kind of submarine, and all sorts of details about the conditions. Then the punch line was one guy says to the other guy, 'Hey, you?' And the other guy says, 'Who, me?' And, of course there were only two guys onboard the submarine, so it had to be him. Dad would laugh and laugh about that joke every time he told it.

He was just a funny, happy man. Even when he was ready for church, he would come in our rooms to make sure we were ready to go. He would break into song and try to get us moving. We would throw shoes at him and he would sing louder. We had a great childhood. Again, I thought everyone lived like we did.

LYNNE'S VOICE

My dad would say:
"Sometimes you just need to do the right thing,
Lynne. Not because you have to; not because you are
required to; but because you need to. It is the right
thing," Lynne Morrow Fruth.

Sometime after Dad had passed, I began to go through his desk. There was a particular drawer, in the top right hand side that was full of just a lot of junk. And I mean there was just all kinds of junk. It was funny because I laughed at the fact that my dad had grown up so poor that he just didn't waste anything. Not a thing. I thought to myself . . . here was a man that was so successful yet he had saved every rubber band, paper clip and spiral notebook—even if there were only two or three sheets of paper that remained. In this particular desk drawer, I started to find notes. Not just one or two, but several notes. These were handwritten thank you notes, from various people, addressing my dad to explain how much what he had done for them had helped them in a dire time of need. He had note after note stashed away documenting remembrances of his giving nature. It made me pause and recall the scripture: and when you do something don't go out and tell about it. Don't let the right hand know what the left hand is doing.

Then I recalled when Dad died, all these people had begun to show up at the house. They shared remembrances of his giving nature with us. It was comforting, confirming and sort of surprising. Not surprising that my dad would have done such things, but that there were so many and from people that I didn't even know that he knew. That happened several times in my life—more reasons why I was always so proud of my dad. For example: I stopped into a tax office in Hurricane one year to get my taxes done and the tax preparer said, 'Oh, your last name is Fruth. Do you know Jack Fruth?' I said, 'Yea, he's my dad!' So then she said, 'Let me tell you a story about him.' It went like this: she and her husband lived right behind the drugstore in Point Pleasant several years prior. They were in the drugstore everyday for one thing or another. One day her husband got the news that he had lost his job. She was so concerned about what they would do and how they would do it. She was in the drugstore and saw my dad. She told him what had happened and he then told her that he knew a person downtown that may just be looking for some help with tax preparation. He told her to go on home and ask her husband, Bill, if he could call downtown and tell them that Jack Fruth sent him for work. So he did. Bill got the job. And thirty years later the husband and wife have their own business doing taxes for folks. And did mine that day. She said that her family would never forget what my dad did for them that day in the pharmacy. He redirected her tragedy. And I thought what a blessing this is to me. After thirty years, somebody stops me and shares this wonderful story. It's like the blessing comes back each time I hear about something that my dad did for someone else.

Regarding the years during which he grew up, things were tough. I think the things that stand out the most to me in terms of the things that Dad talked about were his dislike for blue jeans, pumping his own gas and mowing grass. He wore a lot of blue jeans, pumped a bunch of gas at his parent's business and mowed a ton of grass in Buffalo, West Virginia for extra money.

I did hear many stories about his tap dancing too. He was famous! He and his sister, Henrietta, took a lot of tap lessons and would tap dance at shows all around the area. Dad had the entire outfit from the top hat to the silk suit. At ten years old, his parents would take him to places like Charleston for shows.

Jack Fruth

He was quite good. So later on, he always enjoyed dancing. He and my mother took a lot of dance lessons. Particularly, ballroom dance lessons because he loved that style. And one of the sweetest things to come full circle for him was when he danced with my daughter, Nicole, on one of the last cruise trips we took together. There was a club on the ship and the dance music endlessly played. He and Nicole danced and danced that night. Dad really enjoyed dancing with his granddaughter that night while having the entire family there to see.

Dad worked a lot; consequently he was often away from home. We always had the opportunity to visit him at the store, during the day. And we did often. But when he was home, he WAS home. He was all kind of fun. My mother was not much for getting in the game. She was more nurturing and less involved in the activities outside the home. She was terrified of the water and not interested in swimming. She would grudgingly do it but really it just scared her. Dad was the one who would take us to the creek. We loved it! One of the stories that we often talk about is when we all went to the 'old town' creek with our bamboo poles. I probably wasn't more than five or six years old. Carol would recall this same incident because it was just something we all remembered. We were at the creek with Dad, all five of us kids. We fished with bamboo poles so you just swung them out and hoped the bait stayed on the line and in the water long enough to get a bite or two. I caught the biggest fish! This was the biggest fish that I have ever caught in my entire life up until even now! And I am screaming my head off for Dad! "DAD, DAD, DAD!" Of course, everybody comes running over and Dad is trying to wrestle this huge—I don't know—carp out of the creek and up the muddy bank. Of course all five of us kids are going wild. Dad is on his own with his hands full. We had never seen a fish like that—ever. This fish was as round as it was long, shaped like a milk jug and orange. I can still picture it in my mind's eye. A big ol' orange carp! Dad got this fish onto the bank, after what seemed like an eternity. And you know in my mind we were going to take this fish home. I was going to show everybody this huge fish that

I had caught. Dad got the hook out of the fish's mouth and then all you heard was *bloop, bloop, flop, flop.* It had just rolled back down the muddy bank and back into the creek. Just like that. I was upset! I can still remember Dad said, "Now, honey, you know that I am sure that big fish was the granddaddy of all the fish in the entire creek, even the whole world and it would have really been bad if we would have taken him away from his family. And that was the way he consoled me for losing the biggest fish that I ever caught in my entire life. But I have never forgotten that day. Dad just made things okay. Though I was upset, he calmed me and made everything better again. My sister, Carol, remembers the big fish story—it was one of those childhood things that sticks with you.

The other thing that Dad would always do around the house was he instilled a little spirit of business in us. We were always thinking up ways to make money. From miniature golf courses in the backyard to selling lemonade in the neighborhood, we were out there. Dad had the soda fountain at the store, so he would hook us up with the optimal supplies—the real stuff. That was a lot of fun.

I played a lot of softball. I mean a lot! And my parents went to a lot of my games. I was a hothead! Something had happened to spark my temper. I got irate! Dad pulled me aside and said, 'Until you learn how to control your mouth and your temper, you will never be the player that you have the potential to be.' He told me to stop yelling at my teammates, my coaches and just stop fussing with everybody involved. He told me to shut up and play! He used to say to me, 'No stick, a little glove and a lot of mouth!' And it was true. Though that is how he described me on more than one occasion as a softball player, he was always there in my support.

And support he did. My parents took me to Jerry West Basketball Camp and they gave me every opportunity that was available to further my athletic interests. At that time, there were not many for girls. In 1974, Title-9 came in and the next week my mom and dad went to visit the Mason County Board of Education. He came home that night and said you need to get your basketball out and practice because they will be having a girl's team at Point Pleasant. He made sure that the Mason County school kids had the opportunity to enjoy school sports—both girls and boys. When I graduated high school, I was torn with the decision of which direction to go. My dad said, 'You know if you go to WVU, a division one school and play sports, then you've really done something.' So I did. I didn't make the basketball team, but I did make the softball team. I received a scholarship to play ball. I said to somebody, 'Do you know what? My problem is that I think that I can do anything.' I really think that is the part that I inherited from both my mother and dad. I would rather think that I could do everything and be wrong part of the time rather than think that I can do nothing and be right all the time. There are two kinds of regrets. One kind of regret is: I wish that I *wouldn't* have done that—eww I have a few of those. The second kind of regret is: I wish I *would* have done that—those are the most painful ones. Those are the ones when you do not have the courage to try—the "what if" ones. I look at my dad and know that he made something out of nothing—so I try. You know what? You miss one hundred percent of the balls that you do not swing at.

I recall a time that was particularly etched in my memory when Dad had the store downtown, City Pharmacy. It burned in 1969. We were in school that day. I was in the 4th grade, I believe. That was the day that Mother had promised to take my brothers, sisters and me to the fish store and get a light for our fish tank. The tank was our shared hobby. This light was around twenty to thirty dollars—fairly expensive. We had waited some length of time up to a few months or so. The day had arrived. So I am on the playground at school, as were Carol and John. Mike and Joan were in high school. I remember Carol finding me and saying the store is on fire. All the kids started talking about it. They were saying that hairspray cans were blowing up and the fire was big. All that I could think about was my dad. Where was he? Was he in there trying to get stuff out? Was he in there by himself? Was he okay? All these things run through your mind. Later, after school, we went downtown. The fire was out. It burned two businesses beside it. I can still remember standing there with my coat on looking at some little pine trees that were in round planters out front. The water had been pouring over them and had now frozen. It was all just burned up. I didn't realize until many years later that the business was probably worth a lot and it was basically uninsured. It was a huge financial loss for my parents. The next day my mother took us to get the light. And when we went to the fish store the guy said, 'I cannot believe you guys came to pick up this light.' He thought we would be grieving over the fire. My mother spoke up and said, 'Well you know we promised the children that we were going to get this light, at this time. So we are.' And you do not realize until you are all grown up how that was twenty to thirty dollars that they did not have. Instead of my parents saying, 'Kids, we cannot afford this due to the fire.' We got it anyway. I shared that story in a meeting one time. That fire would have been equivalent to losing a million dollars today, but my parents endured it. My mother had a lot of endurance.

I absolutely tell people that I had the perfect childhood. I had a charmed life. I had parents that loved one another and us kids. They were wonderful. The extended family, the Rossi's and the Crooks' were wonderful. We had aunts, uncles and grandparents. It was just all good. That foundation was built on a rock. All of that family stability and sense of who you are and what your worth is—your value as a person and all that has become a place that I can go to in times of strife and trials. Though I struggle and have heartache, I can always go to that reserve and dig deep for support. It is always there. For some people, they don't have that foundation. Dad did. He had a mother that absolutely doted on and adored him. He had three sisters who unconditionally loved him and he returned the same. He had that strong foundation of love and acceptance, one built on a rock. I think it gave him this springboard to allow him to try and try again until it was right.

As far as business advice is concerned, one thing he would always say was, 'Once you make a deal, you never look back.' He would always say what is done is done. If something went triple in price the day afterward, then it didn't matter. It was done. Don't look back because the future is all that moves forward. My dad was very balanced in his business life and his personal life. He was great at both.

He rarely angered, but did on occasion. He was just wise. He rationalized things well. He taught me that there are those times when you need to do the right thing; not because you are required to; but because you just need to. Are we obligated legally to do this? No. Are we being forced to do this? No. But we do need to. It's the right thing.

My dad really came into his own as a grandfather. So much of what he missed out on as a father by working so much he could enjoy as a grandparent. My girls spent a lot of time with him. We went out for a little while one evening and Dad wanted to stay home and watch Nicole. She was in diapers. Though my dad had five children of his own, he had never changed a diaper in his life. We came back and Dad was so proud of himself! He had changed his very first diaper. We had to investigate his work. Though it was on backwards, it was attached and seemed to be doing the job. We all laughed! He was a terrific grandfather. He taught most of the grandchildren how to swim. He and they enjoyed that, none more than the other. He got to see Nicole graduate from college. He was very proud of her. He died the following year. He was our "go to" guy. That's what I miss the most—our rock filled with all the answers to all the questions to put all the problems at peace. That was what my dad did. I am and will always be so very proud to say Jack Fruth was my dad.

[Lynne Morrow Fruth graduated from West Virginia University with a Bachelor of Science degree as well as a Masters from Marshall University. Though her primary career has been in education, she is currently the President and Chairman of the Board of Fruth Pharmacy, Inc.]

JOHN'S VOICE

"I know that my dad accomplished many things in business, but I have come to most appreciate his love for family, his compassion for people and his service to his church and community. When he is your dad, you don't quite know that he is different from anyone else. In retrospect, I know he really was—different. He did so much for others," John Rothgeb Fruth.

While growing up in Point Pleasant, my brother, sisters and I spent a lot of time at the pharmacy. We referred to it as—the store. As kids, there were three ways for us to get to the store on our bikes. The first option was through the Ordnance Elementary schoolyard, the hard route. It was overlaid with uneven terrain—our bikes would bump all over the place and the grass grew in tall clumps. It just posed the most difficulty through which to travel. We didn't like it. The second option was to ride our bikes along the main highway. We knew we were not allowed to have our bikes on the highway because there was too much traffic. If we did, we would get in trouble because Grandmother would invariably see us when we were half way there with no apparent, alternate escape route. Barring getting caught, this was the easy route. The third option was to take Lincoln Avenue, the scary route. We didn't like this one. It had a haunted house (we were sure this to be true), a bully (he hijacked me and my bike one day and made me take him somewhere) and all sorts of unsightly things that made this our least favorite passage. Deciding which route to take each time we set out to travel those five blocks to the store was a concern for us. Mom would prepare Dad food and we were the delivery service. He worked alone for years and couldn't leave for lunch or dinner. We enjoyed the adventure.

The store was always interesting. Carol was right—there was the time when I swung the gallon of cough syrup around and around enough times until the lid fell off. Sticky syrup ran down my coat and onto the floor. One time Lynne was curious about how much insulation there was between the plastic coating and the phone line and squeezed the scissors too tightly—clipped it right in half. At the time, Dad only had two phones coming into the store. It is true that Dad never asked us to leave though, not once. Not that we didn't get in trouble. We did.

Although my parents and siblings moved many times, we only moved twice while I was growing up. The first home I lived in for twelve years. The second is the home in which my mom still resides. We moved there in 1972. We played in the woods, the vacant lot behind the house consisting of about ten trees. We had a shuffleboard court in the backyard. I thought everyone did. I later found that to be unique. There was a lot of construction going on in Point Pleasant at the time. New houses were being built throughout the neighborhoods. This provided interesting props for us to use for projects. We became carpenters—using leftover lumber and miscellaneous scraps with which to build things. We were climbers—using the huge dirt piles as mountains of unexplored terrain. And jumpers—to see how high up we could go which was quickly followed by how far down we could land. We were kids, invincible. I did take a hit from a hatchet once during the construction of our miniature golf course. I imagine it was Lynne's idea to build the course. She was the planner. We were going to charge the other kids in the neighborhood to play. I was scooping out a tunnel and she was using a hatchet while digging a sand trap. She chopped me, accidently. Our neighbor, Mrs. Casto provided more than one compress to us. I recall her house had a lot of white inside. It was always in pristine condition. Here we kids were scurrying in, dirty from our day's work and bleeding from any one of various injuries. She still took care of us.

While growing up, we played a lot of board games and cards. There were two classic card games: fantan (the game with the sevens) and thirty one (the one that was easy). We were just at Mom's over the weekend and celebrated her eighty-third birthday. It's funny, with all the options of things available with which to celebrate her birthday, we wanted to play cards together. So we did. I have great memories of our family gathered on holidays to play cards at the house. The aunts, uncles and cousins would be there. We would say, 'What does the winner get? What does the winner get?' Dad would say, 'Well a crocheted bicycle of course!' That was the traditional booby prize that he always liked to offer up for the winner—a crocheted bicycle.

Dad did everything, in the early days, for the store. He would come home from work, eat dinner and visit with us for a while. Later, he would pull out his stack of cardboard signs and a magic marker. He would handwrite the advertisements for the upcoming sale—everything from hairspray to paper towels. The next morning, he would gather them, go back to work and hang them in the appropriate spot. He just did everything.

My favorite thing to do at the store was read Spider-Man comic books. I would dart in, say hello to Dad and make a beeline for the bookrack. I was about six or seven years old when I discovered comics. I loved the colorful pictures. With a Reese's Peanut Butter Cup in one hand and a Spider-Man comic in the other, I was set. Any empty spot along a wall or display made the perfect backrest. I would spend hours there. I became a big collector and still have them today. I haven't looked at them in years.

We would often play upstairs in the store too. There were all sorts of spaces to explore. We would lug wheelchairs up the stairs and have races from one end of the building to the other. I bet we made a lot of noise up there. Once or twice I took a friend up there. I got in trouble for that. I suppose Dad thought is was fine for us to be there, but not always a good idea to bring other kids into our mayhem.

When we got old enough, we could work at the store. I enjoyed working in the lay-a-way department at Christmastime. Customers would come to the counter requesting their package(s) to be retrieved and I would go search and then return with them. And if they wanted their package wrapped, that was even better. I enjoyed gift-wrapping and still do. Some people dread it, but I don't. We had this bow maker at the store. It was great. You would first select your ribbon, then load the spool on the machine and turn the hand crank to make as big a bow as you wanted. I thought it was great. Aunt Katy (dad's sister Kathryn) logged my hours. She was the secretary. She did the bank deposits and worked everyday until she was in her late eighties. Aunt Henrietta did the taxes for Dad. Grandmother would do the paperwork and all sorts of things. They were always there, very close—Dad wanted it that way.

When I got older, the person that I was the closest to in the store was Roger Putney. He worked in the camera department. We sold everything to do with photography, from cameras to film developing services. Roger was great for the job. He was good to the customers and had a respectable knowledge of photography and cameras. In Junior and Senior High School, I played tennis. Roger, my brother Mike, and I would often play together. He was a good guy. About ten years ago, we went to his photography studio and he took a family portrait of us. It was good to see him.

Our vacations growing up consisted of trips to state parks. We covered them all, from Pipestem to Glades Springs. Dad loved to be outside, near nature. Most kids went to the beach during the summer—not us. He wasn't comfortable there because he didn't like the heat. We would stay in a cabin, do a lot of fishing and enjoy the company. Dad worked a lot. It was great to have him available all day, everyday for a week. Later in years, we took two family cruise trips. Dad enjoyed a good meal. He would dress in a tie and dinner jacket and look forward to a menu filled with tasty choices. A good sit down meal—he would call it. I recall we were ordering food and Dad had been studying the choices for a while. The waitress came to the table to take our orders. She got around to Dad and he asked her, 'What is the difference between home fries and hash browns?' If he had a choice of one or the other then he needed to know what the difference was. After thinking about it for a minute, she said, 'Actually, there is no difference.' He said, 'Then, I will have that one.' She said, 'Which one?' He said, 'It doesn't matter if there is no difference.' He had a sense of humor—we all laughed.

My dad was a joking person but he was undeniably a man of his word. I was talking to Don Pullin one time and we were discussing Dad. Don told me about a time when the two were involved in a business deal. They were purchasing the records for a pharmacy. They had made the deal and signed the contracts. Dad had spent a great deal of money for this purchase. In finalizing the legal work for the deal, they learned that the seller had not been forthright with accurate information. They were paying too much for something that had little value. Dad could have cancelled the deal. After Dad considered the situation, he decided to complete the transaction. After all, he had agreed to do the deal. If he backed out, what stood to differentiate him from the seller? His word was extended—he stood by it. My dad was a good businessman. When it's your dad, you don't quite know that he is different from anyone else. But he was—different. He did so much for others.

Partly because he had spent so many years doing so much for others, Mom wanted a special place for Dad to have as an escape. A place filled with all the things that he so enjoyed: nature, a pond that invites fishing, plenty of space for family and friends to join and actually just a retreat for relaxation and enjoyment. She knew he needed it. They began looking and in doing so found the cabin and property at Jackson Lake. Though when it came time to buy the place Dad was apprehensive, Mom wanted it. It was just far enough away to be an escape, but close enough to be accessible. She took it on as her project, with his blessing. It became our respite. We would all meet there and visit. Dad ended up loving it there. As he got older, he worked less and fished more. I was never interested in fishing but my boys were. They enjoyed fishing with Dad. We were on our way down one summer to stay at the cabin and we stopped at a fishing supply shop. My youngest son, Alex, wanted to find something interesting to add to the tackle box—just something new with which to fish. He found this enormous fishing lure. It was a big plastic thing with hooks coming out of every available space. He wanted it. We get there and Alex is eager to show Dad his new find. My dad was a conservative fisherman. He would use ordinary night crawlers most all of the time, nothing artificial. He was known for using chicken livers to set his traps for catfish. That was the only time he deviated from night crawlers. So the time came for Alex to cast his line. He was ready. He tried to cast it out but it was heavy. He got it out there and it landed in the lily pads. He stood and patiently waited. After a time, he started pulling on his line and couldn't get it to budge. We thought it was stuck on a lily pad, until we went to help. He had the biggest fish of the day on the end of his line! Neither Dad nor I could have been more surprised. Alex was beside himself with excitement. That lure was enormous. We have many wonderful family memories of fishing with Dad.

My dad was a conservative man in many ways—his home, his things. Material things were just not important to him, not at all. I recall him telling me about how he learned to play chess. He was attending the Greenbrier Military School and traveling home for visits was not an option. Money was tight. He was homesick. He found out that the school had a chess team. And if the chess team was good enough to make the championships they would be permitted to compete in a tournament that was being held in Charleston, West Virginia. So Dad joined the team, of course. He worked hard to learn and then improve his chess game. He accompanied his fellow team members to Charleston and in doing so maneuvered a visit with his family. Dad would say, 'I didn't grow up poor. We just didn't have any money. I never missed a meal. And I always had my family.'

[John Rothgeb Fruth graduated in 1982 from Rose-Hulman Institute of Technology with a degree in Electrical Engineering. John is an accomplished inventor and holds eight patents and two defensive publications. In doing so, he qualified for induction into the Delphi Inventor Hall of Fame. John currently works for Delphi, in the area of semiconductor design for automotive electronics, and has been doing so since graduation.]

A Few Friends
And Colleagues

"Greater love hath no man than this, that a man lay down his life for his friends." John 15:13 KJV

In sharing the life of Jack Fruth with you, there are times when the words from a close friend or colleague prove to offer the best insight into his journey. He had such a vast impact on so many through the years, and here are just a few words from some of his most special friends and colleagues. We begin with Gerry Bosworth.

A FEW WORDS FROM GERALDINE "GERRY" BOSWORTH

"Jack Fruth was a great friend, a respectable person and a refined man," Gerry Bosworth[32].

I first met Jack when he moved to Buffalo, West Virginia. We were about twelve or thirteen years old and in the seventh grade. He was immediately one of our favorites. He fit right in and was loved by all of us. We didn't change classrooms in those days. Our studies were completed together in a one-room schoolhouse. As I recall, Jack was very studious and polite. And he had the cutest smile ever. Jack was a diplomat. When a fellow classmate would have a spat about something or another, Jack would be right there trying to smooth it over. He could not stand for any of us to have a disagreement—he was the peacekeeper. It must have helped that he had that sweet smile.

My late husband, Robert Bosworth, and I were school sweethearts from the time we were nine years old. We would spend our time, while at school and after, with Jack and James Jackson. The four of us were great friends. During those days,

---

[32] *I would like to extend a special thank you to E'Deana Bosworth-Elmer, the daughter of Robert and Gerry Bosworth, for facilitating these words from her mother.*

we rode bikes and fished a lot. Those were our favorite things to do together. On weekends, we would go roller-skating. Jack was a wonderful skater. After skating on a Saturday night, we would all go to Fanny's Kitchen in Buffalo to have a Coke. That Coke was a big deal! To afford a treat like that on any day was very special, but on Saturday night it was even better—a great luxury. Sometimes we would go to the riverbank to sit and watch the water traffic pass. My husband and Jack loved West Virginia and the river. We spent many evenings on the water's edge planning, dreaming and looking forward to our futures. In the innocence of our youth and regardless of our backgrounds, we had big hopes. We just all grew up together from a very modest start.

My husband and I moved to Point Pleasant and lived with his mother on Third Street when we first married. He gifted me one additional rose for each year we were married. The bundle of roses totaled sixty-three, on the last anniversary we shared. We were fortunate to have enjoyed so many years together.

When Jack returned to Point Pleasant with Babs to open their first store, Robert and I were very excited. We were right there to support them. And, as a matter of fact, our family continues to support Fruth Pharmacy today.

Through the years, we would have parties on the river. We would decorate a barge with tables, lights, have music and serve food. And then push it with a towboat along the river. Jack and Babs would get there early, if not first. It gave us a chance to catch up before the business of the party started. I think the world of Babs. She and Jack were perfect for each other. Robert and I always looked forward to seeing them. Our friendship has lasted our lifetimes. All of us enjoyed being on or near the river. It was where we were raised, we dreamed and we lived.

A Visit With
Laddie Burdette

*"I attribute everything material that I have in my
life to Mr. Fruth. He gave me my first job and it
lasted more than thirty years. He was a loyal person
and a great man,"* Laddie Burdette, R.Ph.

I had the privilege of meeting Mr. Fruth in the summer of 1976.
I was studying pharmacy at West Virginia University and looking
for a summer job. Mr. Fruth had earned a reputation of running
a respectable store with a strong pharmacy department. I wanted
to work there. Mr. Fruth invited me back to his office and
introduced me to his mother. I started the following Monday.
It was the beginning of a life-long friendship resulting in nearly
everything that I am today. His moral character and advice was
second to none.

As the days of my summer employment passed, I worked at
the Point Pleasant store with Mr. Fruth. I watched him practice
pharmacy and learned from his example. The time had arrived for
me to begin my official internship to earn the necessary hours for
my graduation requirements from pharmacy school. Mr. Fruth
didn't have an intern position available. However, store #3 had
recently opened in Gallipolis, Ohio under the leadership of Don
Pullin and there was an opening there. I started there full-time in

1979 and worked alongside Don everyday. Mr. Fruth was growing his business and taking people along on his journey. New stores were opening in various locations. One of the next to open was in Milton, West Virginia. Mr. Fruth made me an offer. He said, "You have this opportunity of sharing in up to one-half ownership of the store, getting the store ready to open and managing it afterwards." I had just graduated from pharmacy school. My family had never had debt. My parents lived by the pay as you go plan. I bought my first car when I graduated pharmacy school and paid cash for it with my work money from years past. So to consider the thought of taking on debt was nearly inconceivable. Did I tell you how much it was? It was seventy-five thousand dollars. I talked to my parents about it. It seemed "undoable" for me. It was 1982. I was very young. And it was a large amount of money. Mr. Fruth sat me down for a talk. He said, "Mr. Burdette (as he always called me and I called him Mr. Fruth—never Jack), this is a good opportunity for you." He kept a straight face this entire time. He said, "This is the beginning of something with great potential. If it doesn't make it, what have you lost? It's only money!" Then he lost his straight face and laughed that big, heart-hearty laugh that he had. His entire body shook and his face turned red. I did it; I borrowed the money. That was a long time ago. And you know what? Everything material that I have in my life today is because of that man. Working for him was the first job that I ever had. I trusted him. If he were still with us today, I would have remained loyal to him for all of my working days. He was like a father to me and he treated me like a son.

Much like a father directed a son, he approached me one day to say, "Mr. Burdette, we have a pharmacy intern, Karen, from Buffalo and I think she would be perfect for you." He was a bit of a matchmaker. He thought that I should ask her out on a date. I went to the pharmacy one afternoon in Point Pleasant where she was working. I was talking to her and Mr. Fruth walked in and said, "Have you asked her out yet?" Of course, I turned three shades of red and he got a big laugh out of that one. He and Karen were close friends; they sure thought a lot of each other. At that time, we had business meetings in what was the old Peoples Bank. One evening I waited for everyone else to leave and then I asked Mr. Fruth if he would do me the honor of being my best man. My dad had passed away one year before Karen and I married. Mr. Fruth agreed to do it. He was a compassionate man—not a hard man. He was not afraid to show his emotion.

I would go to him for advice about so many things. When I had a problem, I would step into his office. I would unload the burden in search of a reasonable solution. He would begin to tell me a story. This story would be filled with all these details about who, what, when and where. Most importantly, he would arrive at a potential outcome—an example of what could happen, given the situation. He would never make your decision for you. What he would do is let you leave his office knowing what direction to go in. You felt comforted by his words and confident in his direction. I could have talked with him forever. His interest in the well being of others had no limits. For example, there was a Fruth associate that had worked for the company for years. His wife worked in one of the stores, as well. They had gotten into some serious financial trouble that resulted in bankruptcy. Mr. Fruth had somehow heard of their struggles. So he called the associate into his office, sat him down and offered counsel. He sincerely wanted to lift this man's financial worries. Not to say that he gave him money. He did not. With consent of the associate, he assigned the company accountant, Bob Messick, to manage their income and debts until they were on their feet. He took his personal time and resources to offer help to a struggling family because he truly cared about their welfare. And it's funny, in that same week that Mr. Fruth had this associate in the office, he had the Governor of West Virginia in there too. The governor was seeking advice, so he landed his helicopter at the Armory in Point Pleasant (next door to the corporate office) and paid a visit to Mr. Fruth. Everyone was just a person to Mr. Fruth with merit and matter; his counsel was for anyone and everyone.

I learned from Mr. Fruth by example. He was a person that wanted to do the right thing. In 1990, we went to Charleston to buy a small independent, Oakwood Pharmacy. We had agreed on the purchase price, the amount of inventory that was supposed to be there and a dollar figure for the value of the goodwill of the business. We arrived and walked inside. There was hardly anything there. We had hired an inventory company, RGIS, to do the numbers. There were literally two to three pills in stock bottles on the pharmacy shelves. I mean bottle after bottle, shelf after shelf—very little. I was anxious. Mr. Fruth said, "Mr. Burdette, lets go to lunch." We did. I said, 'Mr. Fruth, what they said was here is not. We have every right to walk away from this deal.' He said, "If we do walk away, they will go bankrupt. They have told all their patrons that they have sold their business. We agreed to buy it. That's what we do, Mr. Burdette. We complete the transaction, as we said we would." I listened and learned. He said, "Mr. Burdette, we need to sleep at night, so we do the right thing." Mr. Fruth always did what he believed to be the right thing. In his words, a good deal for you is a good deal for the vendor too. It can never be one-sided. He never took advantage of his position to push for an unfair outcome with any vendor. Never. His business agreements had to profit each side or not at all. Mr. Fruth always guarded against taking a financial gain at the expense of quality too. He had such an innate ability to make the right decisions. He wanted the best price but don't misunderstand. He also knew that you get what you pay for. Lower prices often reflect lower quality products and services and that was never his goal.

I recall when we opened the Belpre store. In those days, we did everything ourselves. Mr. Fruth, Mike Fruth, Don Pullin, Geary

Spencer and I would put hour after hour in working when we opened a new location. These hours were in addition to our hours of responsibilities involved in our daily duties. So on our days off, we would schedule these store openings. We were working at Belpre and under pressure to get things organized and ready for the grand opening. We dealt with K-L (Kauffman-Lattimer which later would become a part of AmerisourceBergen) for our wholesale drug needs. Well, Cardinal and K-L were competitors for our business. The president of Cardinal, Bob Walters, decided to pay Mr. Fruth a visit while we were at the Belpre store. He wanted to personally talk with Mr. Fruth in hopes of persuading him to do his business with them instead of AmerisourceBergen. For some reason, the Cardinal jet was out for service. Bob borrowed OSU's private jet and flew into Parkersburg, West Virginia. That was just a few minutes from the Belpre store. He surprised Mr. Fruth (all of us actually) with his visit. We were working hard with merchandise everywhere waiting to be priced and placed. Mr. Fruth wouldn't stop working long enough to talk business. Bob tried to impress upon Mr. Fruth that he had gone to great lengths to make the trip that day. It didn't affect him. Mr. Fruth was a great judge of a situation. More people would be affected by a delayed opening versus the potential business transaction that may or may not have occurred that day. Again, he always guarded against taking a lesser price at the expense of quality service. His instincts were impeccable. Therefore, he had no problem making his decision. Fruth Pharmacy continued to be customers with K-L and did for years even after the name change to AmerisourceBergen.

We did all sorts of things together. He led and I followed. We went to Chicago once a year for a huge wholesale trade show. Mr. Fruth, Don Pullin, Mike Fruth and I bought everything for the stores. We worked from six o'clock in the morning until late every night. It was hard work and under a time constraint. We stopped long enough to grab a sandwich but that was it. If the vendors had a reception, Mr. Fruth would say, "Boys, this is dinner." So we ate, sat for just long enough to do so and then went back to the show floor to finalize more merchandise purchases. We had all sorts of situations over the years to erupt during those trips. One year a waterline broke at the hotel where we were staying and we were without water. There were snowstorms that made traveling stressful. There were just all sorts of obstacles that looking back just made the trips more interesting. He loved to buy clocks. Not just a few for one or two stores but lots for all the stores. We would spend hours deciding which ones and how many. I looked at more clocks on that first buying trip than I had in my entire life. He was a great merchandiser. He would load us up with an abundance of stuff. He would say, "Boys, I want to find that special item that will make every housewife drop her dishcloth in order to run out and buy one from us!" He loved to say that. He enjoyed what he did and he was great at it.

Another thing we did together was to go on retreats. These were work retreats—cram sessions. Whether we were at his cabin on Jackson Lake, Canaan Valley Resort or another secluded location, we had what he would call thinking sessions. These too were no frills. We put in a lot of long hours on our days off. He never asked me to work extra. I just understood that he always did and that there was always work to be done. The others and I had a responsibility to him and his company to do it. We wanted to. He was loyal to me. I was loyal to him. On these retreats, we would often take loaves of bread and lunchmeat and break only long enough to grab a bite to eat and then continue on. We would brain storm about ways to better serve our customers, potential new locations for stores, remerchandising what we already had and just any ideas that we could toss out there to improve Fruth Pharmacy. He always strived toward improved customer service.

What I want to say about Mr. Fruth is so much more than I have words with which to express. I want to convey that I am honored to have been associated with Mr. Fruth. I feel privileged to be having this opportunity to share just a glimpse into what we shared over the years. Again, there is so much. Above all, Mr. Fruth was a loyal man, a great man and placed his own interests aside for the betterment of his fellowman.

[Laddie Burdette, R.Ph.,[33] graduated from West Virginia University School of Pharmacy in May 1979. He held various positions throughout his over thirty years of employment with Fruth Pharmacy that included: ownership partner in Fruth Pharmacy of Milton, Inc., Director of Pharmacy, Vice President of Pharmacy, Executive Vice President of Fruth Pharmacy, Inc. and President of Fruth Pharmacy, Inc. Laddie served on the Government Affairs and Pharmacy Affairs Committees for the National Association of Chain Drug Stores (NACDS). He served as Director-at-Large for the West Virginia Pharmacist's Association. Laddie served as a member of the American Pharmacist's Association, Ohio Pharmacist's Association and President of the West Virginia NACDS. Laddie is a past recipient of the Bowl of Hygeia Award presented by the West Virginia Pharmacist's Association. He served ten years on the West Virginia State Board of Pharmacy. Laddie is a twenty-year member and past president of the West Virginia Retailers Association and the past Chairman of the Putnam County Chamber of Commerce.]

---

[33]   *As of the date on which this book is written, Laddie Burdette, R.Ph., works for the Kmart Corporation.*

A Meeting With
Charles Lanham

"When I think of Jack Fruth, I immediately think
of intelligence, ambition, fairness, honesty and
much concern for fellow men and women," Charles
Lanham.

At the end of 1962, I had a change of employment which brought me to Point Pleasant from Ripley, West Virginia. Banking has been my lifelong career. I first met Jack Fruth in January of 1963. He was active in the community. It did not take long for our paths to cross on several occasions. Jack served on the board of directors for Pleasant Valley Hospital, along with Jack Buxton and Shorty Hartley. These were three successful businessmen in Point Pleasant. I worked for Citizens National Bank. We needed to expand the capital account of the bank. So we made the decision to sell some stock in the bank. We invited Jack and Shorty to purchase shares. They did. I often joked with Jack about it, in later years. You see he and his family started their own bank, Peoples Bank, that is now City Holding. I would say to him that the only fault that I could find with him as a person was he put his money in the wrong bank! We laughed about that a lot. It all worked out fine. We shared many board meetings for various councils and foundations and we became great friends.

He had the ability to analyze a controversial situation and arrive at an acceptable solution for all parties. He never took advantage of a situation, even though he often had the opportunity. It was Jack who convinced me to join as a member of the Board of Trustees at Rio Grande University. We had some interesting negotiations through the years. There were difficult decisions to be made with a number of differing opinions. Jack would take his seat, as we all did, then it would begin. Voices would get loud but not Jack's. Bodies would begin to shuffle about but not Jack's. There were times when I looked his way and wondered if he was even awake! He would remain calm as if nothing were going on around him. Sometimes it seemed that he was not paying the least bit of attention. Then, when all was exhausted and a reasonable solution seemed out of reach, Jack would speak up to say, "Maybe we should do this—." Two things would happen. First, it would be a workable and good solution. Second, it would be something that calmed all of us down and people would accept it. Jack had a true gift.

In the late 1960s, the board members of Pleasant Valley Hospital decided they needed to add forty more beds. The forty beds they had were just not enough for Jack. He thought that if the community was going to grow, then they deserved an accommodative health care facility. At the time there were only nineteen of the current forty beds in use but that did not deter Jack. Accordingly, they needed money to expand. They came to us, Citizens National Bank, being the lead bank in town. But we didn't have enough funds to back the project. That did not deter Jack either. He asked us to find it. So we did. He just had a gift about him and he was very convincing. We reached out to a bigger bank to back us and were able to get what Jack needed for the forty-bed expansion project. He was not a quitter.

With regard to the Route 35 project, I feel confident in saying that if Jack Fruth were still living today the highway would be completed. He just had the drive, commitment and resources with which to get things accomplished. His intentions were of the purest nature and his heart was bigger than all of Mason County combined. He wanted a better state of living for his fellow men, women and children.

When I think of Jack Fruth, I immediately think of intelligence, ambition, fairness, honesty and much concern for fellow men and women. He had all those endearing qualities. He is missed much both professionally and personally. His death was a great loss to our community. Jack really was our advocate.

[Charles C. Lanham graduated from Ripley High School in 1946. He is a graduate of Marshall University class of 1952. He holds degrees from the West Virginia School of Banking in 1956, the Graduate School of Consumer Banking of the University of Virginia in 1958, the Graduate School of Banking at the University of Wisconsin in 1962 and the Senior Bank Officer of Harvard University in 1968. He served as co-chairman of the Route 35 Committee for Mason County. Among many other levels of optimum achievements, Mr. Lanham was appointed in 2004 to the West Virginia Senate from the fourth senatorial district, served on the Senate committees on Banking and Insurance, Economic Development, Government Organization, the Judiciary and Labor and Pensions. He has served our local community for years. His level of commitment to community service has not gone unnoticed or unappreciated.]

A Visit With
Ruth Kinnard

I worked many years for Fruth Pharmacy. I suppose you could say that I was the first official pharmacy technician at the Point Pleasant store. Working with Mr. Fruth was a rewarding experience. At that time, the pharmacist did everything for the pharmacy department. Mr. Fruth decided what was going to be on sale, prepared the ad and hung the signs. Mr. Fruth handled all the drug reps that visited the pharmacy. He just did everything. As his technician I was responsible for recording the dispensed prescriptions on the patient's profile card. We kept paper cards in alphabetical order in file boxes on a shelf. Each time a prescription was filled, I would go to the file and retrieve their card. We kept a Rolodex with current prices for each drug, most often in quantities of thirty, sixty and one hundred. I would write the name, strength and quantity of the drug on the card followed by the date and price. After the drug was counted, Mr. Fruth or I would type the prescription label for the vial on the typewriter. We used a Bates Stamper to imprint the label, patient profile card and the original prescription with a matching number for reference purposes. If the numbers were lined up in sequence, which was sometimes difficult to keep in order, we were in good shape. If the prescription had refills, we noted the amount of refills on the profile card as well. Each time the patient returned for a refill, I would pull the card and subtract it from the original number. We had a much different type of operation in those days.

Working with Mr. Fruth, on a daily basis, was a learning experience. If you made an error, he would tell you once and not again. You understood what he expected of you. His pet peeve was finding bottles with lids off. When you finished counting, he wanted that lid immediately put back on the stock bottle. You were not supposed to label the vial or go another step without putting that lid back on first. I recall, he corrected Laddie Burdette for that in the early years. I get tickled thinking about it. Laddie would leave the lids off and Mr. Fruth would be right there after him. Laddie was a good man too.

We got the first computer system in the early 1980s and I was scared to death of it. Computers have really changed the way the pharmacy is run today. It's funny really because it seemed we hired more help after the computers came along. It was supposed to be the opposite. I worked with Bernie Smith, R.Ph. and Don Pullin, R.Ph. in those early years. Later, I worked with Karen Burdette, R.Ph., Rumsey Oates, R.Ph. and Herb Burfield, R.Ph.

Mr. Fruth was such a tender man. In 1979 my family suffered a serious tragedy. My husband was injured while cutting timber. I missed work more than I was comfortable with. I recall he said, "You do what you have to do for your family, Ruth. Your job will always be here." That meant a lot at the time and even now—I never forgot it. He cared about people's well being. He helped my daughter (Kim) get a job at the bank. She is still there some twenty years later. He always took an interest to look out for other people. I had surgery in 1975 and was in the hospital for several days. Upon my recovery, I was offered a job in the insurance business for an increased rate of pay. I called Mr. Fruth to let him know. It wasn't long before he came into my hospital room to discuss it in person. He cared enough to do things like that. I remained as a loyal Fruth employee.

Years later it came time to get certified as a pharmacy technician. It was not required at that time, but looked on favorably. I did not want any part of it. I was worried. What if the exam was too difficult for me to pass? What if I couldn't remember what I had studied? Why was this necessary? I had been doing the job for years. I went to Mr. Fruth. He said, "Now Ruth, you never know when you will be *required* to have this certification. Why not go ahead now and get it while it is still voluntary? Take the test and get it over with. I know you can do it without any problem." He was very convincing with his advice. In hesitation and while in a bundle of nerves, I went to Charleston, West Virginia and did it. I received my Certified Pharmacy Technician certificate, on a weekend, in the mail! I was so relieved. I took it to the pharmacy and held it up. I recall that Herb was shocked! I was too, really. Again, Mr. Fruth was right. He had such wisdom and kindness, much more than there are words for me to say. I miss him.

A Talk With Oshel Craigo

"Jack Fruth's word was his bond. Without question, he was a man of his word," Oshel Craigo.

First of all, I would be more than happy to talk about Jack Fruth anytime, anywhere. He was a very good friend of mine and a wonderful friend to the residents of Mason County. I believe he put the interest of his country first, his community second, his family third and then his business. He had a way of knowing how things would impact the others; he could envision a chain reaction of events, follow them out in his mind and see those events result in a positive outcome for the largest number of people. He was an incredible example of a human being in its most excellent form. His thought process was amazing.

I served in the United States Senate for twenty-two years and in doing so, I represented Mason County. I love Mason County. Jack loved Mason County. He worked tirelessly to better the place. I recall a time that I drove to Point Pleasant. I was going to build a new bridge to replace the decaying Shadle Bridge. I had everybody that was anybody to show up at this meeting in Point Pleasant. We called the newspaper, chamber of commerce, potential supporters, radio and television stations. I offered-up a flip chart presentation to convince the financial backers to agree that Point Pleasant needed this bridge replaced. I told the local community that I knew we could get the money to build the new bridge. What I did need was their support. Then someone shut off the enthusiasm of the project. Just like that. The chamber of commerce people would not talk about it. I wrote letters to the editor of the Point Pleasant Register, time and time again. I would say, 'I am stuck in the Kanawha River mud.' I had no support whatsoever. What had happened? Who had shut the project down? Why? I had a lot of unanswered questions. Two years passed—nothing happened.

At this time, I hardly knew Jack Fruth. One day I get this call. He says, "Senator, this is Jack Fruth. We must be the dumbest people here in Mason County that you have ever tried to help. You tell me what to do and I will see that it gets done. The good people of Mason County need a new bridge." I told Jack that I had already tried; I had been there, wrote letters to the editor of the newspaper for support and exhausted all I knew to do for the project. But Jack said, "Let me try. Tell me what to do." He was convincing. I told him to put petitions out in his stores and all over the county. He did. And do you know what happened? Within a week, Jack Fruth had twelve thousand signatures to support a new bridge! I had never seen anything like it. He took over the shepherding of the new bridge project. He enlisted Charlie Lanham and off they went full speed. From my position as Senator at that time, I wanted an official word of intent from the Governor to finalize things. Arch Moore was running against Gaston Caperton at the time. I invited Arch Moore to affirm the project for Mason County. He couldn't make it but Bill Ritchie represented him. Mr. Ritchie said, "If you want a new bridge, you can have one." Well the election was still ongoing. Considering that, I thought it was important to ask Gaston Caperton for his affirmation for the project as well. I requested an appointment with him. He agreed. At first he said, "I know my opponent agreed to build your bridge in Mason County but I just don't know that I could. To be honest there may not be funding for the project." Anytime you consider the construction of something of such magnitude as a bridge to cross a river, it comes at a high cost; he was right. His career manager at that time was Lloyd Jackson. He was our friend and he helped. He spoke up to say, "Gaston, these people did not travel all the way here from Mason County for you to say that you cannot build their bridge." Jack had a few words to say and was very convincing—that didn't hurt the situation. Before it was over, Gaston Caperton put his arm around Jack and said, "Okay, okay. I still do not know how we will do it, but we will. Your Mason County can have a new bridge." The last official act that Gaston Caperton did before leaving office was breaking ground for the new bridge across the Kanawha River for the residents of Mason County. It took a long time and a lot of work. But it was needed. Gaston Caperton kept his word to Jack Fruth. And Jack continued to serve his community.

In truth, Jack Fruth was the most loving individual that I have ever met; he was such a giving person. He was so tuned-in, so smart and had unbelievable instincts. As a businessman myself, I would consult him for direction. I run Gino's Pizza and Tudor's Biscuit World and he has helped me more than once throughout the years. I would call to ask him how I should do something or sometimes how I shouldn't do it. He always had a reasonable answer. Today I am on the board at City National Bank. That is because of Jack. He did so much for so many of us.

When the consideration came up years ago to build a jail in Mason County, I called Jack for his blessing. The county needed one. I wanted to help build it. Jails on the other hand are controversial facilities. Some neighborhoods just do not want them. Jack wanted things in Mason County. He knew it would create jobs for the local people and generate revenue. He told me who to call—and it was done.

He initiated the construction of the Marshall University Mid-Ohio Valley Center Off-Campus facility in Point Pleasant. He wanted it there for the local residents to have educational opportunities close to home. And again with the addition of such a facility, the county would generate jobs and create cash flow in and out of his community. He initiated the construction of the Mason County Health Department. His work with the development of Pleasant Valley Hospital was ongoing for years. I could say it time and time again and I will because it is the truth. He did so much for his community and with only the intention of bettering the lives of his fellowman. He was a man of great compassion for others.

[Oshel B. Craigo attended West Virginia State College (business) and is a licensed real estate broker in the State of West Virginia. Mr. Craigo is the Owner and CEO of Better Foods, Inc., Gino's Distributing, Inc., Craigo Real Estate and several additional companies. In addition, Mr. Craigo served in the West Virginia Legislature for twenty-two years and served on committees, including the Banking and Insurance Committee. He was the Vice-Chair of the West Virginia Senate Finance Committee and for eight years was Chairman of the Senate Finance Committee. Mr. Craigo is active in civic and community affairs and serves on several boards and committees including: the Board of Directors for the National Restaurant Association, Chairman for the West Virginia State Tourism Committee, Vice Chair of the Board of Directors of Charleston Area Medical Center, Teays Valley Hospital and Chairman of the Putnam County Democratic Executive Committee.]

REFLECTIONS FROM BERNIE SMITH

"I feel very blessed to have known Jack Fruth and to him I say, thanks for the memories!" Bernie Smith, R.Ph., MBA, MHA

I first met Jack Fruth at West Virginia University (WVU) School of Pharmacy in 1965. He and Bill Hockenberry came to WVU to recruit me to go to work for him when I graduated in 1967. I had gotten married, during those last two years of school to another pharmacist, Beverly, so he agreed to hire both of us. I had one summer of experience with Rite Aid but knew very little about the retail business in general. I had lived on a farm all my life and was skilled in raising strawberries, shearing sheep and putting up hay. None of those tasks translated into retail business experience. Jack gave me an opportunity to learn and grow with him.

Jack had two stores in Point Pleasant. At that time, there was one downtown on Main Street and one big store uptown on Jackson Avenue. I was placed in the store downtown along with Bill Hockenberry. My wife, Beverly, was placed in the one uptown. This was the beginning of my retail business learning adventure. Jack and his family were well known in Mason County, so most of the population came to one of his stores for their prescription services. Jimmy Hall, R.Ph. had Hall's Drug Store downtown on

Main Street as well. But it seemed he did little to promote the store; therefore, it offered little competition to Jack.

One of the first lessons that I learned from Jack early on was about people. He knew how to treat people with respect, both employees and customers. The employees of Fruth Pharmacy were very loyal to Jack. They always addressed him as Mr. Fruth. He treated them fairly and respected their contributions to his stores. He taught me that if you treated those who work for you with respect, then in return they would work hard for you everyday. I still practice that lesson today with the eighty employees in the long-term care pharmacy that I manage. He also expected his employees to treat the customer in a first class manner, making sure they had a good shopping experience while visiting Fruth Pharmacy. He promoted his people skills and in doing so relayed them to others.

Another thing Jack taught me was how to use advertising as a means to grow the business. We were always looking to bring new merchandise into the stores and then to promote it through the local newspaper. He had special sales, with good prices, throughout the year. The public looked forward to shopping at Fruth Pharmacy for bargains. He would also schedule sidewalk sales on a yearly basis. Those were his way of ridding a lot of leftover inventory from the stores. Jack knew how to move merchandise. The time had come to expand the scope of advertising. We made the decision and developed our own circular and in doing so made it a monthly event. It was a huge success. In my opinion, that was most likely one of the tactics that led to the expansion of the Fruth chain. Jack was always thinking of ways to promote the store. Christmastime was big and busy. We always tried to beat the previous year's sales. Jack used loss leaders (items that were sold at cost or a little below) to attract customers into the store. He knew once they were inside they would buy something else because the store was jam-packed with merchandise. Fruth Pharmacy had everything and Jack Fruth knew how to sell it!

Jack was also a master of finance. He along with some of his friends and relatives had started People's Bank in Point Pleasant. Since he was one of the members of the Board of Directors, he had an easy supply of money with which to buy merchandise. This led to another lesson he taught me, about cash flow. I learned the importance of cash flow and how to incorporate that lesson into the daily business flow. I also learned how to buy merchandise on credit and use the company's money instead of my own. And I learned the importance of company discounts when paying for merchandise. Jack was truly a master at making money work for him and his business. I learned so much from him through the years.

I spent ten years working for Jack before leaving to pursue my own business ownership career. In retrospect, it may have been a mistake on my part and his. But at the same time it seemed like the right thing to do.

My separation from Fruth Pharmacy left me as a business competitor. Jack and I had several battles. I believe we were both upset with each other on several occasions. But we continued to remain close friends at all times. He taught me to separate business from friendship and that friendship was the more important of the two. Being a competitor of Jack taught me how to better negotiate and find other more creative niches by which to attract customers. Today I still harbor all those skills and utilize my ability to grow a business using the experiences taught by and learned from Jack Fruth.

During the years spent with Jack, my most disappointing experience was being told that I was not going to be a part of the Fruth chain after I sold my business back to him. I believe Jack realized it later but at the time was influenced otherwise by his employees. Regardless, it did not hamper my career. I took my experiences and lessons from Jack Fruth and today I manage a multimillion-dollar company. And I do so for the second greatest entrepreneur that I have ever encountered in my professional career. Jack Fruth was the first. I feel very blessed to have known Jack Fruth and to him I say, thanks for the memories!

[Bernie Smith, R.Ph., graduated in 1967 from West Virginia University with a Bachelors of Science in Pharmacy, in 1983 with a Masters in Business Administration from Ohio University, in 1991 with a Masters in Health Care Administration from the West Virginia Graduate College Institute with additional electives in Managed Care and Rural Health Care in West Virginia. Bernie is a registered pharmacist in the states of West Virginia and North Carolina. He is also a licensed West Virginia Nursing Home Administrator. Bernie was appointed as a member of the West Virginia Medicaid Drug Utilization Review Board for the Department of Health and Human Services in March of 1993. Bernie is the recipient of West Virginia Health Care Association Distinguished Service Award for 1998, Past Master of Point Pleasant Minturn Lodge #19 and Past Patron of Point Pleasant Chapter #75 Order of the Eastern Star.]

A Visit With Ruth Flowers

I had the opportunity to sit for a visit with Ruth Flowers. We met at the corporate office. She was candid with her thoughts and it was obvious that she had a great love for Jack Fruth. Her admiration was not only for him but also extended to his wife, Babs, and the Fruth children. She wasn't comfortable with the tape recorder turned on, so she talked and I took notes. We shared an hour together and during that time, this is what Ruth had to say—with much emotion.

Fruth Pharmacy, Jack Fruth and the Fruth family have been so much a part of my life for so long that I can't remember being without them. He was one of the greatest people that I ever had the privilege of knowing. As a boss, he was great! As a listener, he was great! As a businessman, he was the best! I used to tease him and say that he could take a nickel and in five minutes make five thousand dollars with it! He was modest though—very humble. He would call me Ruthie. The family calls me Ruthie. They are all good people.

While the kids were growing up, Mr. Fruth was very good to my son, Eddie. He fostered Eddie, really. We actually met through the boys. The youngest Fruth child, John, and my son were the same age. They played sports together, tennis as I recall. In understanding that not all children get to participate in all the things that a parent would like for them to, I would like to say that my son's, Eddie's, childhood was more enriched because of Mr. Fruth's big heart. Eddie was at their house a lot. They took my Eddie on trips with their family and included him as one of their own. Mr. Fruth put me to work all those years ago and I now have twenty-two years in as a loyal Fruth Pharmacy employee. I wouldn't trade a day of it.

He is very missed in the stores. I see problems today, in the pharmacy, that need approached and I automatically think of him. He was the one that I would go to with those types of things. He was always reasonable. He could look at each side rationally and then discern the best outcome. His management skills were fantastic, like nothing I have ever seen. I sure do miss him so very much more than I can say. I find comfort in being at the store on a daily basis. It gives me the opportunity to visit with Babs. She and I have become family over the years. They are one of a kind people.

REMEMBRANCES FROM JAMES "JIM" FARLEY

"Jack Fruth was a bright, intelligent, professional pharmacist and businessman. When he spoke, others listened," Jim Farley.

I was the Hospital Administrator at Pleasant Valley Hospital in Point Pleasant, West Virginia for nine years from January 1971 until December 1979. During that time I was privileged to work closely with Jack Fruth. Jack was one of the members of the Board of Trustees at the hospital where he was the treasurer, chairman of the finance committee and a member of the Executive Committee. Working together we experienced major growth and improvements of hospital services, turning the hospital around from a marginal operation at best, to a thriving asset to the community. Jack Fruth was heavily involved as an active member of the Board and Executive Committee. He had great passion for the local community hospital and worked hard to make it successful. As the Hospital Administrator, I received most of the credit for our success, but the Board of Trustees deserved credit as well and Jack was a key member of the Board during that period of time.

Jack Fruth was a bright and intelligent professional pharmacist and businessman and when he spoke, others listened. He chose the proper time to speak and when he spoke, we listened as he could analyze the situation and come to a very logical and practical conclusion to the matter at hand. He would not dominate the discussion, rather he would organize his thoughts and present his suggestions at the proper time and most often, he was right on target for our decision.

I was a very young Chief Executive Officer with good training in hospital administration, in fact; I was twenty-nine years of age, the youngest Hospital Administrator in the nation. Jack's advice and counsel was very important to me in the first few years as we were making many operational changes that involved many difficult decisions. Jack, along with other Board members such as: Al Biggs, Jack Buxton, Charles Lanham, Rudy Friar, Harry Miller, R. G. Greene and others were very supportive which greatly helped in implementing the needed changes to improve the hospital. We did it as a team.

After nine enjoyable and successful years, I was recruited to start a health care management company in Cincinnati, Ohio and resigned my position at Pleasant Valley Hospital. That was a very difficult decision. Many years have now gone by, but I have never forgotten how blessed and fortunate that I was to have such outstanding people surrounding and supporting me such as Jack Fruth. Upon departing, Jack and I hugged and wished each other well and both expressed our pleasure of having worked with each other during such an important time in the development of Pleasant Valley Hospital.

We often return to West Virginia to visit friends and relatives. While traveling on Route 35 from Point Pleasant to Charleston, I smile when I see the Fruth/Lanham Highway sign and think of those two quality individuals who have done so much for Point Pleasant and Mason County. They also have done a lot for my career and me. Especially, in the early and formative years which have helped me so much. It was such a privilege and honor to work nine years closely with Jack Fruth and Charles Lanham, two good friends to each other; and two people that I greatly admired and respected back then and still do today. It perhaps was the most challenging, happiest and quickest nine years of my adult career and one that I look back upon with such pride of accomplishment. Jack Fruth played such a key role.

[James "Jim" L. Farley of Cincinnati, Ohio is the president, managing partner and co-founder of Nursing Care Management of America Inc., a privately held health care company with ownership and management of long-term care nursing facilities and home health and hospice care companies in several states. He served on the Ohio Health Care Administrators Licensure Board in Columbus for six years, including four years as chairman. The American College of Hospital Executives honored him as the Most Outstanding Young Hospital Administrator, in the nation, with the Hudgens Award in 1977. Jim served on the board of the American College of Health Care Administrators for 10 years and was elected national president and chairman of that organization, serving from 1989 to 1990. In southwest Ohio, he assisted several universities with their health care administration programs, including service on the advisory boards of Xavier University and the University of Cincinnati and as a lecturer and preceptor at Miami University. Jim is highly active in civic and community organizations; he served as president of his local Chamber of Commerce, a bank director, and a member of the Rotary Club. Farley has served in many capacities as a volunteer in the tennis community at the local, regional and national levels. He served as president of the Greater Cincinnati Tennis Association for four years and chaired various committees of the GCTA, the Ohio Valley Tennis Association and the USTA/Midwest Tennis Association. In 2010, Farley was elected to the International Tennis Hall of Fame Board of Directors and in 1990, the Jim and Bobbie Farley family was selected by the United State Tennis Association as the National Tennis Family of the Year.][34]

---

[34] *Special thanks to HNN proved by Marshall University*

MEMORIES SHARED BY PASTOR STEVEN E. DORSEY

I was privileged to serve as the Pastor of the Trinity United Methodist Church from June 1986 to June 1999. In that time, Jack Fruth was the chairman of our finance committee and a very active and faithful member of our family of faith. The Jack Fruth that I knew was a humble and caring man. He not only loved his Lord but he also loved his church. He was a man whose heart was as big and generous as anyone I have ever known. There was never a cause or a need in the life of our church or community that Jack did not support. But he never wanted any recognition or fanfare. He just quietly went about using his resources to help others.

Jack Fruth wasn't a very tall man but he was a giant of a man when it came to getting things done. As chairman of our finance committee for many years, he was instrumental in helping to guide and promote the ministry and mission of Trinity Church over the years. As one of the leaders on our building committee for the new addition, it was Jack Fruth's confidence and faith in our congregation that "sold us" on the idea that we could accomplish anything as a church that we set out to do. It was Jack Fruth and "Shorty" Hartley who organized and set out a workable financial plan to accomplish what turned out to be a million dollar addition. It was Jack Fruth and many others who worked behind the scenes to take this vision and develop it into a plan and convince our people that it could be done. It was Jack Fruth who sat in on all those planning meetings with the architect and made suggestions so that our church would be able to meet the challenges in the new century, as far as our facility was concerned. It was the positive leadership and forward thinking of Jack Fruth that was instrumental in bringing this new addition into being. And yet, Jack would be the first to say, "It was all of us working together that made this project so successful."

Jack was very much at ease talking to governors, congressmen, community leaders and just plain folks. He would take the time out of his busy schedule to share a word of advice and I always felt comfortable stopping by the corporate headquarters to talk to Jack and ask his opinion about things. He loved his family and he delighted being around his children and grandchildren. I would often see him stop by and eat lunch with his sister Kathryn Fruth or stop and talk with his sister Henrietta Rossi. He loved and valued his family and he never forgot his roots.

The day of his funeral was on Saturday, July 23, 2005. I remember it being very hot and the sanctuary was full of family, friends and fellow church members. The thing that I remember the most occurred just following the funeral service. As the processional traveled north through Point Pleasant on the way to the cemetery there were hundreds of people standing along the roadside out of respect to this wonderful gentleman. What a touching gesture of respect and love for a man who truly made a difference in the Point Pleasant area. Yes, Jack Fruth truly made a difference in the life of our church, in building up educational opportunities in the community, in strengthening the business climate of our state, in working to improve roads and bridges in Mason County and in serving the public through the Fruth Pharmacy. It was truly a privilege to have known Jack Fruth.

[Steven E. Dorsey is serving his eleventh year as senior pastor of Bridgeport United Methodist Church in Bridgeport, WV. A graduate of Huntington East High School in Huntington, WV, Rev. Dorsey received a Bachelor of Science Degree from Marshall University, Huntington, WV; and a Master of Divinity Degree from Duke Divinity School, Duke University, Durham, NC. Prior to coming to Bridgeport UMC, Rev. Dorsey served Trinity UMC, Bluefield, WV; Athens UMC, Athens, WV; Duff Street UMC, Clarksburg, WV; and Trinity UMC, Point Pleasant, WV. He and his wife, Jennie, have three adult children—S. Elliott Dorsey, Jr., Thomas Earl Dorsey, and Mary Margaret Dorsey. They are also the proud grandparents of one grandson—Benjamin Case Dorsey.]

FOND MEMORIES FROM C.K. BABCOCK

"The world seldom sees such a kind, understanding and respectful soul as Mr. Fruth. It saddens me to consider how much worse off the world is without him," C.K. Babcock, PharmD, CDE

My story about Mr. Fruth begins well before I ever met him. During my first year of pharmacy school at WVU, I started working at the Fruth in Eleanor, West Virginia as a pharmacy intern. While at the Eleanor store, I was taught many aspects of the way Fruth Pharmacy operated; including what was expected of employees in order to uphold the Fruth name. It became apparent that Kevin and Jada (the pharmacists there) had great respect for Laddie Burdette. At that time, he was Vice President of Pharmacy and therefore supervised all the pharmacists in the chain. Laddie had hired me as an intern. It didn't take long for me to understand why Kevin and Jada held Laddie in such high regard. I began to recognize a pattern of respectable people along the steps leading to Mr. Fruth.

At store level, Mr. Fruth was highly admired. It was evident that through the years he had taken risks with his company in order to provide us with a decent place to work. We understood the extent of his loyalty and we reciprocated. Mr. Fruth was well known to us as a man who led by example, with integrity. He thanked us for taking care of our communities. We thanked him for the opportunity to do so. The graceful pattern of his layered integrity became more apparent to me. It was almost impossible to believe at first. How could one man truly be so intelligent, respectable, humble and brave? Not to mention that he was from West Virginia and my employer. There's more. After four years working at store level, my role changed with Fruth Pharmacy. I signed-on to do a residency at the corporate office but I had not yet met Mr. Fruth.

My residency began and a month or two had gone by. I had seen Mr. Fruth in passing and in doing so we only had the opportunity to exchange hellos. During those first couple of months, however I did learn why the other pharmacists held Laddie in such respect. He led by example, as he had learned from Mr. Fruth and I noticed how he treated all Fruth employees with respect. An outward pattern of professionalism seemed to grow stronger and stronger the closer I got to Mr. Fruth at the corporate level. Laddie would take on task after task and in doing so make the best out of every situation, especially the worst ones. Laddie was now President of the Company and Eric Lambert (a pharmacist as well) was the Director of Pharmacy. I continued to see a pattern. First, Laddie had joined the company to follow the leadership of Mr. Fruth. Later, Kevin (my mentor) and Eric had joined because of their esteem for Laddie. This continued to enforce my thoughts about the quality of character of Mr. Fruth. If all these good men were working for this company because they respected and admired Mr. Fruth, he must be impressive indeed.

It was late one evening and I was working. It was usually Eric and me busy in our offices until well after dark. The stores are open until 9:00 pm, so many times it was helpful for us to be available to take calls, answer questions, solve problems; basically be there in support of our Fruth employees who were working late in the stores. I didn't know anyone else, aside from Eric and me, was still there. Mr. Fruth popped his head in my doorway and asked me to join him in his office after I finished what I was working on. Mr. Fruth was working late, too! Here was the man, Mr. Fruth, working. He didn't have to be there but he came in everyday. When I reflect on him being there, I recall that everyone noticed his presence. He spoke to everyone. As a matter of fact he didn't speak at them, but with them, considerately. Not the typical owner of a one-hundred million dollar company who had his name on everything from stores to stationary and held more awards that I ever knew existed. I nervously gathered myself and started toward his office. I thought I was walking down the hallway of my doom. I had only been working in this position for two months. I thought I was doing okay—well even. But what if it wasn't good enough? He had high standards. During those few seconds that it took me to nearly run to his office, I had all sorts of thoughts pouring through my mind. Was he going to say that I would make a good pharmacist someday, but not today? Was he going to say that I wasn't living up to his expectations at the corporate level? I just had no idea what I was walking into. With a deep breath, I slowed my pace. I anticipated this to be pretty quick. If he was as good as I had come to believe, he may even make it fairly painless. I walked into his office. 'Yes, sir?' I said. He smiled, looked at me and said, "Take a seat." In his voice of unexplainable comfort, he said that he just hadn't had the opportunity to get to know me. We proceeded to chat which emulsified into a visit. After a half hour, I wasn't sure what was actually transpiring but I felt safe. I felt he could have led me into a fire and I would not have flinched. As a matter of fact, I would have even wanted to go in. I left his office, ran down the hallway and all the while was amazed that I was still employed! I now understand that he was simply getting to know me, personally. He was making sure that his employees and customers were in caring hands. He had more style and grace than any one person I had ever met.

Those evening conversations became common, but I wish we could have had more. We talked about stories of the wants of youth—he was curious about my generation and our expectations in life. He told tales of age and wisdom. He was a most impressive man. I found out quickly that he did not have to put on airs to let me know it either. He was simply Mr. Fruth and that said it all. In all honesty, he exceeded everything that anyone had ever said about him. I enjoyed our visits in his office, looked forward to them and miss them today.

Mr. Fruth helped pattern me into the man that I am. He had started it before I met him, indirectly through Laddie, Eric and the pharmacists at Eleanor. Through the years, he directly strengthened it though our personal relationship. After he passed away, he continued to do so. In knowing he had been a Freemason, I was encouraged to learn more about the organization. And through his memorable example, I became a Freemason myself. To say the effects of Mr. Fruth resound with me today and always will, is not only true but also is the reflection of a blessed journey. I feel very fortunate to have been a part of his life.

[C.K. Babcock[35], PharmD is a graduate of the West Virginia University School of Pharmacy, Doctor of Pharmacy degree. He is a Certified Diabetes Educator and is licensed to practice pharmacy in both West Virginia and Ohio. C.K. completed a community pharmacy practice residency with Fruth Pharmacy, Inc., under the direction of Eric Lambert, R.Ph. Throughout his many years of service to Fruth Pharmacy, C.K. held various positions including: Pharmacist-in-Charge, Director of Pharmacy, Director of Clinical Services and Director of Staff Pharmacists. Today, C.K. is a Clinical Assistant Professor at the West Virginia University School of Pharmacy in Charleston, West Virginia. His professional affiliations include: West Virginia Pharmacist

---

[35]   *As of the date on which this book is written, C.K. Babcock, PharmD, CDE works for the West Virginia University School of Pharmacy.*

Association Board Member, National Community Pharmacist Association (NCPA), American Diabetes Association (ADA) and the American Association of Diabetes Educators (AADE). In 2005, C.K. was the recipient of the Distinguished Young Pharmacist Award from the West Virginia Pharmacist Association (WVPA). In 2006, he was the recipient of the Young Pharmacist of the Year Award from West Virginia Society of Health System Pharmacists (WVSHP).]

The Impact Of
Mr. Jack E. Fruth
On The Lives Around Him
From
Dallas Kayser

*"And now these three remain: faith, hope and love.
But the greatest of these is love."* 1Cor 13:13 (NIV)

When Angie Johnson first asked if I would like to write some comments about the impact of Jack Fruth on the lives of those who knew him, I was delighted. After all, I had worked with Jack in many different capacities since 1977, as his attorney, at our bank, hospital and church, and had the privilege of seeing him in action and watching closely the impact he made on others' lives.

But when I tried to summarize my personal reflections on Jack's influence on others, I quickly decided that to summarize anything about the impact on others of Mr. Fruth in a few short words would be next to impossible. Of all the amazing traits that Mr. Fruth exemplified: intelligence, kindness, business savvy, entrepreneurial talent and so many others, the most striking to me was his love for his wife, Frances, his children, his faith, his work and co-workers and his community.

Early during my nearly 30 years of working with Mr. Fruth, I remember watching he and Frances (Babs) together at a Christmas party for the employees of the Peoples Bank of Point Pleasant (one of the institutions that Mr. Fruth founded with a few other businessmen in the community), and how stricken I was with the love they showed for one another. It was really fun watching Jack and Frances dance and otherwise be together in just about any setting. They were best friends and Jack often credited Frances with many of his own successes. What a neat role model they were for married couples of today!

Not only in personal settings, but also his love and caring for others shone through in business settings as well. To observe and listen to Mr. Fruth in group meetings where difficult issues were addressed was another true learning experience about Jack's concern for others. Jack had the uncanny ability to take an issue with many complex parts, simplify the issues into one big picture and make recommendations to the others present that resulted in solution after solution. Never, however, did he recommend a solution that would bring hardship or misery on others. He would do nothing to solve a significant business problem by inflicting unemployment or other economic hardship on those who worked with him. People really did not work for Mr. Fruth, they worked with him, and his love for them showed in this type of problem solving.

And his love for all those he cared for, his church and faith, kept Mr. Fruth leading by example until the day he passed on. He worked to make this community a better one, and he did that by loving those around him and living that love in the actions that he took and the lifestyle he led. To this day, we who worked with Jack wish he were still here to help lead us through decisions we are now required to make without his guidance. We would and should honor his memory by acting upon and utilizing the same loving principles he exhibited in making tough decisions in our community and world today. I, among so many others, am thankful for his life and his example.

[Dallas Kayser is a 1973 Summa Cum Laude graduate of Marshall University with a Bachelor of Arts degree in Economics and earned a Juris Doctor degree from the West Virginia University College of Law in 1976. In law school, he served as an Associate Editor of the West Virginia Law Review and was honored with selection to Order of the Coif, the most prestigious award given to law students. Dallas entered the practice of law in 1976, practicing in Huntington, West Virginia and Point Pleasant, West Virginia. In 1979, he founded the Law Offices of C. Dallas Kayser, L.C., the predecessor of Kayser Layne & Clark, PLLC.]

A Message From Mario Liberatore

"So the Lord spoke to Moses face to face, as a man speaks to his friend." Exodus 33:11

The first time I met Jack Fruth was on December 13, 1967, two days before the Silver Bridge fell. It was early in my professional career and I was interested in the potential for an opportunity to advance. I had heard of Peoples Bank, which was a new bank that had been started by Jack and a few others, in what was then the growing and developing town of Point Pleasant. I was hesitant to consider the change at first, but I decided to make the trip from Man, West Virginia for the job interview. After all it was not only an opportunity to explore an untrod challenge but also to start on the ground level of a newly established bank. I was scheduled to interview with Vitus (Shorty) Hartley. He was one of the original founders of the bank, along with Jack and a few others. Shorty and I sat and talked, got acquainted and then we talked more. It must have gone successfully because the next thing I knew we were on our way to meet Jack at his store, Fruth Pharmacy. At that time I still wasn't sure that I wanted to leave my present job in Man and relocate to Point Pleasant, West Virginia. At least that was until I met Jack Fruth in person. Once I met Jack, I was one hundred percent sure that I would accept the offer. During our

197

short visit, he impressed me as a man of good character, a man that I could trust. I took the job that day and I have never left Point Pleasant since.

What I didn't know then was how much of an impact that Jack would have on my life, both personally and professionally, for many years to come. Personally, I feel in having known Jack Fruth that I am a better person. Professionally, I had the opportunity to accompany Jack in many meetings throughout the years. I learned very quickly that he had the ability to analyze any situation and then make an accurate decision that best fit a positive, productive outcome. He did this more quickly than anyone I have ever encountered—time and time again. His insight into problem solving and his adeptness to do so was remarkable. He had the clearest vision of any person that I have ever met.

Though I have many fond memories of Jack Fruth, many more than I can recite, what I vividly recall is the manner in which he always treated people with respect. Jack had a great love for both family and community. I've never met another man like him.

[Mario Liberatore is a graduate of Marshall University. He served as the President of Bank One from 1994 to 1997, at which time he joined Ohio Valley Bank and has since remained. He is the Senior Vice President of the Ohio Valley Bank Holding Company and Chairman of the West Virginia Bank Group. In addition to Mario's work at Ohio Valley Bank, he is heavily involved with his local community. His servitude extends to the Main Street in Point Pleasant Committee, Mason County Community Foundation, Pleasant Valley Hospital, Rotary, Mason County Area Chamber of Commerce, Marshall University Advisory Board, Point Pleasant Junior and Senior High School Athletic Complex Committee and the Marshall Mid-Ohio Valley Center (MOVC).]

Remembrances From Eric Lambert

"Go therefore and make disciples of all nations, baptizing them in the name of the Father and of the Son and of the Holy Spirit, teaching them to observe all that I have commanded you. And behold, I am with you always, to the end of the age." Matthew 28:19-20

The first Fruth Pharmacy that I remember going into was the one in Milton, West Virginia. I wasn't very old, about thirteen. While waiting on my parents to get prescriptions filled, I explored the store and found all kinds of interesting things. Between looking at the magazines, toys, knives and video games, that ten or fifteen minutes quickly passed. My parents would track me down and out the door we went. While attending Milton Junior and Senior High School, my friends and I would often walk to Fruth to get candy and pop. We also left with other items, from time-to-time, that were not quite so innocuous like water balloons with which we returned to school. Fruth Pharmacy was just a part of our community, a part of our daily routine.

While on semester break from my freshman year of college, during the winter of 1987, my parents and I stopped in at the Hurricane Fruth. It had just opened. We were looking around the new store when I recognized Laddie Burdette, R.Ph. was working in the pharmacy. We knew him because he had been our pharmacist at the Milton Fruth for years. Since the store was new and I would need a job come summer, I asked Laddie if he had anything available. I let him know that I could work at either store, Milton or Hurricane. He said, "Yes. Stop in, Eric, when you are out of school and I'll put you to work." I thought, how easy was that? He knew us from the Milton store but that was it. That seemingly simple decision on Laddie's behalf resulted in a life changing direction for me both personally and professionally. And, for that I am forever grateful.

When I returned from a less than stellar first year of college, I started working at both Fruth in Milton and Hurricane in May of 1988. I worked in many different areas of the stores, including: gifts, cashiering, back stock, maintenance and pharmacy technician. It was through my work at those stores and my assisting on new store construction that I grew to not only know and appreciate Mr. Fruth but also to admire him.

With no idea what direction I was going in when I started working that summer, I found solace at Fruth. I had just dropped out of engineering at Virginia Tech and was undecided about my future plans. There was one thing that I did know and that was I enjoyed working at Fruth Pharmacy. I decided to take classes at Marshall University in the fall while working. I first met Mr. Fruth at the Hurricane store while he was visiting with Laddie one day. I had heard great things about him—he seemed like a larger than life figure to me. I was impressed with how he seemed so nice, modest and certain that things would work out for the best. Though I did not have day-to-day contact with Mr. Fruth, I learned that those qualities which made him successful obviously were present in Laddie Burdette, Geary Spencer, David Jenkins, Bob Wiseman, John Donahue and many others that he entrusted to help manage his operations and run his stores.

My life began to get exciting—college was falling into place and I loved working at Fruth. In the beginning, I was given the opportunity to have a job. The longer that I stayed and worked it seemed the job turned into the opportunity. Fruth was expanding and I had the chance to assist in store remodels, relocations and the set-up of new builds. I enjoyed all these new challenges. Laddie continued to be supportive and encouraging, a mentor. He told be about his history of working with Mr. Fruth when he was starting out. With his direction, I decided that going to pharmacy school was the thing for me to do.

Mr. Fruth gave me the opportunity to go to pharmacy school. He made me an offer of one thousand five hundred dollars per semester to attend West Virginia University School of Pharmacy. All he asked in return was that I work that same amount of time for Fruth upon graduation, as repayment. I could not think of another place or any other people that I would rather work at or with so I promptly accepted. In addition to this, both Mr. Fruth and Laddie Burdette wrote letters of recommendation for me. I am certain that those letters were the deciding factors in my admission to the school of pharmacy. And, do you know what? Mr. Fruth was even nice enough to write me a letter of congratulations upon my acceptance. It was overwhelming to me that man of that magnitude was even aware that I existed—let alone take the time to wish me well in pharmacy school. Fruth let me work as much or as little as I wanted throughout the next several years. I cycled through my clinical rotations throughout West Virginia. The minute I mentioned that I worked for Fruth, everyone commented on what great men both Mr. Fruth and Laddie were.

Upon my graduation, the Milton store had an opening for a pharmacist. How cool was that? The very store in which I had grown up, in the town where I attended school for six years and the one where I knew the people in the community. That was perfect. Fruth had held that opening for me for several months awaiting my graduation. It was a fun store in which to work. Mr. Fruth and Laddie allowed me to practice pharmacy, as I saw fit as they did most all the pharmacists that they hired. They took an interest in their employees. They trusted the ones they chose. Mr. Fruth and Laddie encouraged doing things for the community as a way to return goodwill. I agreed with them. I visited schools and gave talks, answered questions at library events and senior citizen centers. I joined the local Lions Club. Both, Mr. Fruth and Laddie always encouraged me to do what was best for the patient and everything else would work out fine.

Mr. Fruth told me to get involved with the profession of pharmacy. He encouraged me to join the West Virginia Pharmacist's Association (WVPA). He felt it was important to stay up on current changes in the practice of pharmacy. Under his direction, I became an active preceptor for pharmacy students to help teach them the correct way in which to care for patients. A big opportunity came for me in 1995. Mr. Fruth was chosen by Governor Cecil Underwood to be a part of the West Virginia Medicaid Task Force. Mr. Fruth, who had other obligations, recommended me. I was appointed to the committee representing community pharmacy for West Virginia. This was a great experience. I had the opportunity to see how the inner workings of managed care, Medicaid, generic and brand pharmaceutical lobbying shaped the way in which patients received prescription care and services. This experience allowed me to meet influential people and ultimately led not only to my involvement with WVPA but also my role as President of WVPA in 2004-2005.

At the end of 1999, I was promoted to Director of Pharmacy of Fruth Pharmacy, Inc. I started working at the corporate office in Point Pleasant, West Virginia. While there, I had the opportunity to be involved in important decisions regarding store designs and acquisitions. Another task with which I had the opportunity to be involved was creating and developing new programs that dealt with pharmacy workflow and operations. This was also a time of great networking opportunities. Various pharmaceutical conventions and meetings for organizations such as the National Association of Chain Drug Stores (NACDS) and the National Community Pharmacy Association (NCPA) required travel all over the country. The message here is what Mr. Fruth was doing. He felt strongly about keeping in touch with the heartbeat of the pharmacy profession. Both Mr. Fruth and Laddie were actively involved in numerous professional and civic organizations. I learned by their example.

Mr. Fruth was truly instrumental directly and indirectly on my path of life. Throughout the years he was always there to tender advice on pressing issues or to lend his unique perspective to a given situation. He had such a keen ability to know the best course of action which would lead to the most beneficial outcome for all parties, both sides. He fostered the opportunity to learn and grow, the opportunity to create and build and importance of learned lessons along the way. I feel extremely fortunate to have been involved with the Fruth family. By the Fruth family, I mean every associate that worked at the corporate office and in all twenty-five stores including Mr. Fruth. We were a united group of people focused on optimal customer care just as he had envisioned for our communities. Mr. Fruth's understanding of the right way in which to treat people is one of the most valuable lessons that I learned from my time as a Fruth Pharmacy employee and that was learned that by watching him.

[Eric Lambert,[36] R.Ph., graduated from West Virginia School of Pharmacy in December 1993. Throughout his twenty-two years of service to Fruth Pharmacy, Eric held the positions of Staff Pharmacist, Pharmacist Coordinator, Director of Pharmacy, Director of Pharmaceutical Management and Vice President of Pharmacy. Eric is the recipient of the West Virginia Distinguished Young Pharmacist Award for 2002. He served as President of West Virginia Pharmacist's Association from 2004-2005. Eric holds memberships in the following professional organizations: American Pharmacist's Association, West Virginia Pharmacist's Association, Ohio Pharmacist's Association, National Community Pharmacist's Association and National Association of Chain Drug Stores. Eric was a member of the West Virginia School of Pharmacy Advisory Board. He was a member of the Interviewing Committee for the University of Charleston School of Pharmacy. Throughout his professional years, Eric has served as a preceptor to many pharmacy students from multiple schools of pharmacy.]

---

[36] *As of the date on which this book is written, Eric Lambert, R.Ph., is the Vice President of Operations for healthwarehouse.com located in Florence, Kentucky.*

SHARED
COMMENTS FROM
MICHAEL SELLARDS

"I was privileged to call Jack Fruth my mentor, counselor and friend," Michael Sellards.

In 1982 Jack served as chairman of the Pleasant Valley Hospital board of trustees and chaired the search committee to hire a new Chief Executive Officer (CEO). I applied for the position. In doing so, I participated in several interviews with Jack and other members of the board committee. At the completion of the process, I was invited back to meet with the committee. Jack, as chairman, then offered me the position. As a matter of fact, Jack drawled, 'Michael you can do this job in a half day and what you do with the other twelve hours will be up to you.' That light-hearted story made us all laugh and cemented a professional relationship that lasted the eighteen years that I represented Pleasant Valley Hospital as CEO.

Jack's magic was leadership and vision. He was invaluable to my career and the success of Pleasant Valley Hospital.

[Michael G. Sellards is currently the President and CEO of St. Mary's Medical Center in Huntington, West Virginia.]

A Visit With Two
Of The Fruth
Grandchildren

I had the opportunity to meet with two of the Fruth grandchildren, Nicole and Elizabeth, Lynne's daughters. We met at the corporate office last year,[37] on Lynne's birthday actually—the girls had traveled in to see their mom on her special day. Though they spent much time in the small town of Point Pleasant, while growing up at their grandparent's home, they have made their lives elsewhere. When I say traveled in, they did. Nicole lives in California and Elizabeth (Liz) lives in Florida. It was interesting to talk with them as they recalled their grandfather with much love from a different perspective yet with the same theme as others. The girls expressed a blessed and gifted childhood experience with both grandparents. Though it was obvious they love and miss their grandfather, their admiration for their grandmother was equally apparent.

'Our grandfather loved all of us so much and he was not afraid to show it! By all of us, I mean the big five and the little three. You know who the big five and little three are right? There are two sets of us, grandchildren. I (Liz), my sister (Nicole) and my cousins (Stephanie, Patrick and Chris) make up what our family refers

_____
[37]   *The year being 2010*

to as the big five. We are all one-year apart, stair steps.' Nicole added, 'Now the little three are made up of my two cousin (Alex and Thomas) and my brother (Michael) and they came along eight years later.' Liz laughed and said, 'When our little brother came along, it was like the best present ever! I was obsessed with him and so was Nicole.' As the two sisters sat side-by-side, they spoke. Often at the same time, one was completing the sentences of the other. It was clear they had been close with each other and with their extended Fruth family throughout their childhood.

'Our grandmother was terrified of the water! Oh, she did not like it at all. Which was the opposite of our grandfather. Our grandparents have an in ground pool at their house. Grandfather was the big advocate for that—we wanted it. He would swim and play in the pool with all of us for hours,' Liz recalled. 'Our grandfather taught all of us to swim!' said Nicole.

The girls shared stories about the times they would visit the corporate office to see their grandfather at work. They talked about stopping in his office for a hug and then making their rounds to the conference rooms in search of candy and pop. It seemed they recalled all of their times with him as happy and love-filled. Liz recalled, 'I can only remember him yelling at me once, only one time ever. He only did it because he was worried about me. I was going down a dark path and he knew it. He was very observant. You might first think that he wasn't always paying attention, but he was. For example, he would send us to get Chinese food and give us too much money for it. I mean over hundred dollars at a time, just to get Chinese food. I used to think that he just didn't know how much things were but I was wrong. He knew everything. He was just taking care of us.' Nicole laughed and added, 'I remember the time that he dragged Thomas out of the dining room. That was huge! He never angered about anything but Thomas had misbehaved long enough. Grandfather had a serious talk with him in private. None of us expected that.'

The girls recalled one evening when the University of Rio Grande was having Fruth Pharmacy night. In the name of Fruth Pharmacy, their grandfather had donated much money to the university over the years. He enjoyed attending this event and appreciated that the university was grateful for his generosity. On this night, Nicole had show choir competition. Grandmother said, 'We are going to Nicole's program.' Grandfather said, 'What?' She said, 'That's right, we are going to show choir tonight.' He said, 'But—what? Wait, we could try doing both. We could first go to show choir and then second go late to the Fruth Pharmacy night at the university. Right?' Grandmother said, 'I am going to need to see the results of the show choir competition, which means I am going to need to stay to the end of the event.' He said, 'Well I guess we don't really need to go to Fruth Pharmacy night at Rio Grande this year.' Nicole said, 'They were always at all of my events, that meant a lot to me. I could always count on them to be in the audience. And I was in a bunch of stuff (show choir and three sports). They, my entire family, believed in me—I always had that comfort.' Nicole and Elizabeth sometimes cried and most often laughed as they recalled moments like this with their grandparents—one after the other, each intimate in its own way.

Though I know it would be most difficult to do, for anyone, I asked the girls if they could summarize their grandfather in a few words. I asked the them if they could share what he most meant to them. After a moment or two, a veil of thought covered their faces and tears came to their eyes.

Liz said, 'In my entire life, no matter what happened—no matter what I got myself into—I always knew and will always know how much he loved me, my mom, my siblings, my grandmother, my cousins, my aunts and uncles—all of us! Through all the changes, while growing up and now, there was never a time that

I doubted that. He was the perfect example of a person that lived his beliefs. Whether it was in his business or in his personal life, he gave, gave and gave more. My grandmother was the rock. My grandfather was the pillow. She cooled him down; he warmed her up. Those two were very much in love—a relationship from a storybook. I love him for everything he was.'

Nicole added, 'For me, when thinking about what I should be doing with my life, at a particular time or during a certain stressful turning point, I think of my grandfather. What kind of advice would he offer, if he were still here? I so trusted what he said. He was so humble and honest. His primary purpose was to do good for others. My grandfather made a name for himself and lot of wealth for him and his family by being an upstanding person. He proved that you could become successful by doing the right thing. He always did what was right, no matter the cost. The biggest life lesson he gave me—was through his actions, I was able to see his example of goodness.'

LETTERS FROM A GRANDFATHER TO HIS GRANDDAUGHTERS

"Children's children are a crown to the aged, and parents are the pride of their children." Proverbs 17:6 (NIV)

Lynne shared some personal letters that her dad had written to her daughters a short time before he passed away. Though they could have been retyped, it seemed more appropriate to let his penmanship personally deliver the messages. His love for them is well defined in the advice he offers and through the lessons he shared.

January 5, 2005

Dear Nicole,

This is intended to be a pep talk. I warn you in advance.

I am also enclosing a humorous column which may produce a smile or two.

So let's go.

It is extremely important in your entire life that you always have a positive attitude and decide that you are going to be happy. On stressful days, and stressful times always try to see the humor or the light hearted side of each situation. Remember nothing happens is all good or all bad, so always look for the good, no matter how small. e.g. it is difficult to see the good from something as tragic as the Tsunami event but I am sure there will be some., such as, it unites the people working together to provide food and water for the hundreds of thousands of homeless. They may rebuild many of the destroyed buildings with stronger and safer buildings etc., etc., etc.

Secondly, for your own self esteem, it is extremely important to give 110% to whatever you are doing. Particularly your work, your job, or anything you are receiving a paycheck for — Keep that positive attitude and say to yourself, I may like or not what I'm doing and I may be doing this for a day or a month or many years but while I am — I'm going to give my best.

Thirdly, always know that you can do whatever you decide you want to do, if you want it bad enough and are willing to devote yourself to achieve it.

Nicole, you are one of the most talented, most creative people I have ever known. You are very intelligent, broad knowledge, etc.

The challenge in life is how we use our talents, our intelligence, and our knowledge to not only make us happy, successful, and keep us healthy — but how do we use these traits to make a contribution to society, to strive to make this a better place to live.

The greatest compliment that can be made about you after you are gone is "This is a better place because Nicole was here."

Now, let's talk about your job. Your job fills several specific basic needs because it provides you the means to pay your rent, buy your food and clothes. Hopefully, it also provides you the means for a few luxuries over and above your basic needs. This makes life more pleasant and more enjoyable, and as you progress in your job, more will be available for this purpose.

So, how should you approach your job.

1. You should approach your job as a positive learning opportunity. How will this job further your education and experience so that when you move on to your next challenge you will feel more confident and knowledgable. Just as you look back on show choir, church, school, college and previous jobs and say "Gee, that really taught me how to handle

this situation." So learn all you can while you are there and take advantage of every opportunity to broaden your experiences. Remember, you majored in Religion and Dance but you probably landed your present job because of your experience and knowledge gained on the side by working with the Opera group and W. Va. theatre group.

2. Be patient! Be patient! Be patient!

As smart and great as you are ~ it took <u>four years</u> to get your degree from Oberlin. Don't be discouraged that you're not running the cosmetics department at Macy's after four weeks. (or four months for that matter).

3. Stop worrying about losing your job. Look around you, are you more capable than many of the associates working at your same level. Remember, if you were the supervisor, or department manager ~ would you eliminate the strongest or the weakest person in your department? Think about it! And remember one of my favorite stories ~ Two men were out walking in the woods and they came upon this giant bear. The bear came charging toward them and the two men began to run. The one fellow said "Do you really think you can outrun this bear?" The other replied, "I don't have to outrun the bear ~ all I have to do is outrun you!"

Can you outrun some of the people you work with?   TO BE CONTINUED

1st INSTALLMENT ~ WATCH FOR SECOND INSTALLMENT.

4. Be dependable!

Show up for work every day you are scheduled and be on time. Managers and supervisors love people they can depend on.

Remember when you were running hurdles (shuttle relay). You had to depend on every member of your team. And every member did not have the fastest time. You just needed the fastest time of the four of you totaled up. Many teams may have one person who (or was) is faster than anybody on your team — but is the team faster.

5. Be optimistic and be a winner — my dad taught me that business is always good, he said everybody wants to trade or do business with a winner — nobody wants to deal with a loser.

6. You are being paid and you are being hired to solve problems — not create problems. So constantly ask yourself — "Am I contributing to the solution — or am I creating more problems?" Be a problem solver — not a problem maker.

7. Maintain the ~~proper~~ proper attitude! An attitude that says I want to improve my performance. I am here to learn — I want to do better — I welcome any suggestions that will improve my performance. Ask your supervisors, your associates, and your customers — "How can I improve? What can I do to increase sales? How can I better serve my customers? What are my weaker areas that I need

to improve.

     8. Find out what the company expects from you and do a little more. If they expect you to do 5 make-overs a day — do 6. If they expect 10 — do 11 or 12. etc. Always strive to exceed their expectations.

     9. Accept responsibility for your mistakes and learn from them. Don't blame somebody else for the shortfalls. You never build yourself up by tearing somebody else down. Say, we didn't do as well as we expected, but I learned some things and cite what you learned, and I know I (or we) will do better next time and cite some things you plan to change or improve upon which you believe will guarantee you do better.

     10. Look your best at all times. You're selling cosmetics — use them — you are a walking display. ~~Remember you are a professional.~~

When you ~~en~~ enter a clothing store, if it is a men's store selling expensive suits, every man has on a suit, co-ordinating shirt & tie - shined shoes. He's presenting an image that says "Wouldn't you like to look well dressed like me?" A women's dress shop - all the sales associates wear suitable dresses, etc. Liz wanted to work at one of the mall's teen-age fashion stores. ~~For you~~ A requirement was each clerk had to wear the store's clothes. How many young people walk into that shop and say "OH, I love those jeans (top) (BELT) (SHOES) and where can I get those. Become a walking billboard.

11. FIND Your customers needs and fill them. Talk to your customers. Talk to your customers. Talk to your customers. Why are they here, what are they looking for, knowledge about them is invaluable. What do they like or dislike, what is their hot button. Your mother would buy anything if it was purple (or wrapped in purple). The woman is not coming in to buy a lipstick, she's coming in to buy something to make her lips more attractive. or to create an illusion, a look, match my shoes, purse, or on and on.

She has things about herself she doesn't like or wants to improve, she's not buying a product - she's buying self-esteem - she's buying confidence - she's buying appeal.

You have the knowledge and the experience, If you want to feel great about yourself and your job, help this lady feel better about herself. Compliment her - build her self-esteem (but be honest with her in the process) point out her good features, show her how to best emphasize those and teach her how to use the products you sell her.

If you do a makeover, and the customer is pleased, you are pleased, she goes home or back to work and gets pleasing reactions from her family (spouse), co-workers and friends. Everybody's happy and think what a great service you have performed. That's what it's all about.

12. Don't dwell, fret and worry about your quota. Do your best everyday, and keep improving - sales will take care of themselves. The secret is doing a good job on your makeovers and building your customer base.   TO BE CONTINUED

ELIZABETH

On June 3, 2004, I will be 76. I am in reasonably good health but I am having a very difficult time in my life. I have had a wonderful, wonderful life. I have had a loving wife for almost 54 years. she is ~~one of~~ the sweetest most adorable person I have ever known. Her love for me, her love for her children and her love for her g. andchildren is truly a miracle. She has spent her entire life taking care of my needs, our children's needs and our grandchildrens needs.

I, on the other hand, have spent the last 52 years building FRUTH PHARMACY. I have been successful far beyond my wildest dreams and I have loved my work, loved the people that work with me and loved the people we have served but I am in a state now - how long can I continue in this business, if I sell - probably at least 25 to 35 % or more of the people working for me will not keep their jobs (We employ over 600) What will I do? How long can I continue as we are. I am faced with all these questions and then my closest sister I grew up with died at 77.

I want and pray for all of my children and all of my grandchildren to be healthy and happy. I don't care what you do in life as long as you are happy, you do it honestly and don't harm other people in the process.

ELIZABETH - <u>YOU</u> ARE THE ONLY ONE THAT CAN MAKE <u>YOU</u> HAPPY.

The Third Installment

No. 13. Don't take everything _personal_.!!!.
If you encounter a disgruntled customer,
or a frustrated customer vents upon you,
just listen and be polite, analyze what they
are saying and then determine if it is really
your fault and you really did something wrong
or is this just a frustrated customer yelling and
screaming at you — because you are there and he
can't get to anybody else.

   Let me tell you a story. I was working
in Xenia, Ohio as a pharmacist and asst.
store manager very early in my career. We had
__3__ drug stores in the entire town of Xenia;
ours was in the middle of the block, another
a half block away on the corner, the third
a block away from the corner. One evening
a middle-aged man came in with a prescription
I looked at it and informed him I did not
have that medication in stock but would call
Dayton (about 12 miles away) and have it for
him tomorrow morning. He started ranting
and raying, cussed me out, said he could
drive to Dayton & get it tonight and
loudly proclaimed he had been to 3
pharmacies in town and none of us had it.

   At this I began to smile and merely
listened to him rant and rave because

I now realized — I was his 3rd choice and he probably did not say a word to the 1st or 2nd pharmacist. I was 3rd choice and I catch all the hell — but if No.1 or No.2 had had the medicine — he would not have even gotten to me. I smiled and tried to keep from laughing as he stormed out. Why should I be upset — he was just frustrated because everybody was out — but he didn't get upset with his first choice, or his 2nd choice — just with me because I was his last chance. So just listen, take it in stride and don't take it personal. I felt like telling him that look - if corner pharmacy had had it or XYZ pharmacy down the street - you wouldn't even be in my pharmacy. — Realize that the frustrated customer is upset and it has nothing to do with you personally in most cases — so keep your cool — don't get upset.

On the other hand, if the customer has a problem, you can solve — you may win a customer for life."!! Think about it!! (But don't let it upset you.!!!)

For a homework assignment in 1979, Lynne's daughter, Nicole, was asked to write about the West Virginian she most admired.

Nicole Trovato
Age: 7
Ripley Elementary School
Grade: 2

The West Virginian I admire is my grandpa. I admire him because he can tease me like nobody else can. This is an interview of my grandpa. My grandpa's name is Jack Edward Fruth.

My grandfather's children's names are Mike, Joan, Carol, John and Lynne. His mother's name is Marjorie Rothgeb Fruth. His father's name is Henry Edward Fruth. He was married in 1950 to Frances Elizabeth Fruth.

My grandpa went to Greenbrier Military School when he was fifteen in September of 1946. In that same year, before he went to military school, he got very, very sick with pneumonia and the measles. It made him go blind for three months!

His hobbies (when he was young) were hunting, fishing and tap dancing in shows with one of his three older sisters, Henrietta.

He was born on June 3, 1928. His awards are the Bowl of Hygeia, for outstanding community service as a pharmacist. Another award he won was the award of President of the West Virginia Pharmacy Association. And also is President of the National Association of Chain Drug Stores.

He likes to watch television. He says it's educational and entertaining. The he said that it puts him to sleep.

He was raised with a lot of love and by three older sisters: Henrietta, Emogene and Kathryn. He likes to sleep late on Saturdays and Sundays. He has a favorite chair. His favorite chair is in the living room and he sits in it until it's dinnertime. Then he comes to eat.

What my grandpa hopes to accomplish in the rest of his life is to see all his grandchildren grow up and to see all his children get out of debt.

Jack Edward Fruth
As A Freemason

Jack Fruth was a Freemason, a member of a society of men based on specific moral and spiritual values. It is sometimes referred to as Masonry, and it is one of the oldest fraternal organizations in the world. The West Virginia Masonic Home was established pursuant to a resolution of the Most Worshipful Grand Lodge of Ancient Free and Accepted Masons in the state of West Virginia adopted on November 15, 1917. Located in Parkersburg, the home is under the management of a Board of Governors who are responsible for its operation and the care and maintenance of its residents, under the rules and regulations prescribed by the Grand Lodge. Although there is much mystery and in the past Freemasonry was much more of a secret society, today there is not that much reticence concerning the Masons. Today it is not unusual to see Masons wearing rings, jackets, hats and even sporting bumper stickers with the standard symbol of Freemasonry, the square and compass. Masonic buildings are almost always clearly identified. Though the Freemasons still have some secrets such as passwords and handshakes, there have been many publications throughout the years depicting their practices.

To become a Mason, a man must show himself to be morally and mentally qualified. Freemasonry encourages its members to prize learning and teaches them to be tolerant of others. Masons are to regard each man as their equal and to offer respect and assistance as needed to anyone and everyone. Jack Fruth served as a Freemason for years and took great pride in his membership and encouraged others to follow.

Professional Activities

- Served as President of the West Virginia Pharmacists Association in 1973

- Member of the Ohio State Pharmaceutical Association

- Member of NARD—National Association of Retail Pharmacists

- Served as a Pharmacy Representative to Medical Advisory Board to West Virginia Department of Human Services from 1974-1993 and served as Chairman from 1970-1983

- Served on the Board of Directors for Associated Chain Drug Stores, Inc.

- Served as the National Chairman of Affiliated Associated Drug Stores from 1989-1990

- Served as Director and Member of the Executive Committee as well as the Secretary for the Chain Drug Marketing Association, Inc.

- Member of the West Virginia Board of Pharmacy

- Member of the Ohio State University, College of Pharmacy, Corporate Council

- Member of the West Virginia University College of Pharmacy Visitation Committee

PROFESSIONAL AWARDS

- Bowl of Hygeia Award for Community Service by the West Virginia Pharmacists Association in 1975
- Honorary Master's Degree of Public Service from the University of Rio Grande in 1986
- Mason County Area Chamber of Commerce Community Service Award in 1990
- Chain Drug Marketing Association Hall of Fame Award in 1992
- Distinguished Alumni Award by the College of Pharmacy, Ohio State University in 1993
- James H. Beal Award by the West Virginia Pharmacists Association in 1995
- Who's Who in West Virginia Business in 1995
- Ernst and Young Entrepreneur of the Year in 1999
- West Virginia Entrepreneur of the Year Lifetime Achievement Award in 1999
- Distinguished West Virginian Award by Governor Cecil Underwood in 1999
- Marshall College of Business Hall of Fame 2000

CIVIC AND SOCIAL ACTIVITIES

- Director: Peoples Bank of Point Pleasant, WV beginning in 1965—including Chairman of the Executive Committee from 1965-1988 and Chairman of the Board from 1988-1998

- Director: City Holding Company 1986-1998

- Former Director: Mason County Chamber of Commerce—including serving as President in 1968

- Founder: And, first President of the Hidden Valley County Club in Point Pleasant, West Virginia

- Member: West Virginia Roundtable

- Member: Loyal Order of the Moose

- Member: Trinity United Methodist Church—including Chairman, Finance Committee and Member of the Board

- Member: Point Pleasant Chapter Rotary from 1953-1965—including President in 1962

- Member: Board of Directors for the Green Acres Center for Mentally Retarded from 1960-1967—including Chairman in 1962

- Member: Minturn Lodge No. 19—A.F & A.M.

- Member: Pat Wilson Shrine Club

- Member: Beni Kedem Temple

- Member: Royal Order of Jesters

- Member: Board of Trustees for Pleasant Valley Hospital 1958-2005—including President from 1982-1983

- Member: University of Rio Grande Board of Trustees—including President of the Board of Trustees from 1996-1998

- Member: Chairman of the Board of Directors for Genesis Affiliated Health Services from 1999-2000

- Member: Regional Economic Development Authority of Rio Grande, Ohio

- Vice President: Mason County Development Authority

FRUTH SCHOLARSHIPS

The Fruth family and Fruth Pharmacy, Inc., continues to support local students with generous contributions toward better education, in Jack's absence. Through a multitude of educational facilities, the Fruth Scholarship Funds[38] offer a helping hand to deserving students.

Marshall University
Fruth Pharmacy Scholarships (up to 6)

Established in 1995, this scholarship is awarded to an active employee, or a relative of an active employee of Fruth Pharmacy who is enrolled full or part time at Marshall University. The recipient must maintain a 2.5 grade point average, during their course of study at Marshall University.

~

Jack E. and Frances "Babs" Fruth Scholarship

---

[38] *Scholarship information was provided, in part, via the Fruth Pharmacy website. For more information regarding eligibility opportunities, visit: www. fruthpharmacy.com*

Established in 2000, this scholarship is awarded to a member of the Marshall University Women's Softball Team or another female athlete who is enrolled full time at Marshall University. Preference is given to players from Point Pleasant High School or an athlete from Mason County.

Marshall University Mid-Ohio Valley Center
Jack E. and Frances "Babs" Fruth Scholarship Fund

This scholarship, established in 2000, is restricted to a student studying their first year of college as a full time student at the Marshall University Mid-Ohio Valley Center in Point Pleasant, WV with at least a 2.5 high school grade point average.

Mason County Community Foundation
Jack E. and Frances "Babs" Fruth Scholarship Fund

Following the death of Mr. Fruth, this scholarship was established in 2007 by the community and family donors. The scholarship is awarded to a Mason County High School, West Virginia graduate who will be enrolled full time in an accredited college or university in West Virginia. The candidate may be pursuing either a two-year or a four-year degree. The candidate must have a high school grade point average of 3.5 or above.

Putnam County, West Virginia High Schools
Fruth Pharmacy-Math Field Day Scholarships (5)

～Honoring excellence in Mathematics ～

Beginning with 2011-2012 school year, Fruth Pharmacy will award a $200 scholarship to the top scoring Math Field Day Senior from each of the following schools: Buffalo High School, Hurricane High School, Poca High School, Winfield High School and Teays Valley Christian School. Scores at the County Math Field Day will determine the winners.

～

Ohio State University
Jack and Frances "Babs" Fruth Scholarship Fund (2)

Established in 2001, this is an endowed scholarship with the income providing scholarships to students in good standing interested in community pharmacy with preference to students from West Virginia or the Ohio counties of Washington, Athens, Meigs, Gallia, Jackson, Pike, or Lawrence. The scholarship is typically given to two students each year.

～

University of Charleston School of Pharmacy
Fruth Pharmacy Scholarships (2)

This scholarship was established in 2005 to help young men and women who are pursuing a degree in pharmacy, these scholarships are restricted to students enrolled in the University of Charleston School of Pharmacy in good academic standing.

～

University of Rio Grande
Henry E. and Marjorie M. Fruth Scholarship Fund

Established in 1986, this scholarship is restricted to a student or students from Mason County, West Virginia studying at the University of Rio Grande, in good academic standing.

University of Rio Grande
Jack E. and Frances R. Fruth Scholarship Fund

Established in 1992, this scholarship is awarded to an active employee, or a dependant of an active employee of Fruth Pharmacy who is enrolled full or part time at the University of Rio Grande. The recipient must maintain a 2.5 grade point average, during their course of study at the University of Rio Grande.

West Virginia University
Fruth Pharmacy Scholarships (4)

Established in 1992 by Fruth Pharmacy, this endowed scholarship provides yearly awards to help young men and women who are pursuing a degree in pharmacy. These scholarships are restricted to students enrolled in the WVU School of Pharmacy in good academic standing.

In many ways, I see the manner in which Jack Edward Fruth bestowed his gracious gifts on others as an intimate time between a shepherd and his sheep. With daily attention, he led folks on a journey to higher ground where fresh spring grasses were growing and the heat was not as oppressive, a better place for all. I believe that was Jack Fruth's intention. So at the end of this heartfelt journey through a modest portion of his blessed life, I leave you with this scripture:

Psalm 23
A Psalm of David.
1 The LORD is my shepherd; I shall not want.
2 He maketh me to lie down in green pastures:
he leadeth me beside the still waters.
3 He restoreth my soul: he leadeth me in paths of righteousness
for his name's sake.
4 Yea, though I walk through the valley of the shadow of
death, I will fear no evil: for thou art with me; thy rod and thy
staff
they comfort me.
5 Thou preparest a table before me in the presence of mine
enemies:
thou anointest my head with oil; my cup runneth over.
6 Surely goodness and mercy shall follow me all the days of my
life: and I will dwell in the house of the LORD for ever.

God Bless and Amen
Angie Johnson

Acknowledgments

I would like to tender a warm and gracious thank you to Sandy Keefer. She works at the Fruth corporate office and has done so for years. Each time I needed a photograph, newspaper article or date of importance she saved the day and did so with a smile.

A grateful acknowledgment is offered to Jane Lambert for her willingness to be involved in this project. I not only appreciate her encouragement regarding my efforts toward writing but also her insightful thoughts regarding the content of this book.

I want to thank Eric Lambert for his presence throughout the book. Time and time again he answered countless questions regarding one store or another. I would also like to thank him for offering important contact information that led to a variety of input from other people. And lastly, for the times when I felt this task was greater than the good that I could bring to it, I thank him for encouraging my forward movement toward completion.